Divine Service
A WOMAN'S BIBLE STUDY

BETTY HENDERSON

journeyforth®

Greenville, South Carolina

Cover Photo Credits: istockphoto/spopho

All Scripture is quoted from the Authorized King James Version.

Divine Service: A Women's Bible Study
Betty Henderson

Design and page layout by Peter Crane

© 2010 by BJU Press
Greenville, South Carolina 29614
JourneyForth Books is a division of BJU Press

Printed in the United States of America

ISBN 978-1-60682-158-9

15   14   13   12   11   10   9   8   7   6   5   4   3   2

This book is dedicated to the following servants of the Lord:

Dr. and Mrs. Wendell Heller
Dr. and Mrs. Ben Strohbehn
Dr. and Mrs. Bob Taylor

My husband and I have had the joy of serving Christ with all three of these godly couples. They are humble servants and have shown us, and countless others, what it means to be "fervent in spirit serving the Lord" (Romans 12:11).

Contents

Preface

On June 7, 1618, Pastor George Petters in the county of Sussex, England, began to preach verse-by-verse through the gospel of Mark. He continued preaching weekly from this shortest of the gospels until May 28, 1643! For twenty-five years this faithful pastor dug deeply into every corner of the book's 678 verses. We can only imagine the bountiful food he fed his people during those years. I'm afraid that my digging around in this exciting book for the last several months pales in comparison with Pastor Petters.

When you begin your own digging in these lessons, you may be tempted to accuse the author of being a descendant of Pastor Petters! Some of the lessons are a little longer than others, and for personal or group study you may need to divide some into two studies. It was a little challenging to squeeze sixteen chapters of this wonderful book into twelve lessons. While studying, you will see the richness of the content Mark included while writing under the power of the Holy Spirit. God had given Mark a second chance to serve Him, and it surely delighted his soul to have opportunity to record so many wonderful stories of Jesus.

I have included with each lesson what I call my "Shadow Servant" friends. Over the years I've been privileged, through books, to rub shoulders with these godly men and women. Their life examples have changed my life, and I'm excited for you to meet them. Reading great biographies always affords us opportunities to learn from saints who are now seated at our Lord's right hand. You'll notice that five of my servant friends ministered with Pastor Charles H. Spurgeon. I did not especially single out his ministry in my search for shadow servants, but through the years many of his fellow-laborers' names have been included in the numerous books on his ministry. Thus it is easier to locate the story of their service.

Divine Service

Hanging on the door of every Bible-preaching ministry could be a sign reading "Humble servants needed. Please apply!" These school, church, mission, or camp ministries need young servants, old servants, and every age of persons in between. Are you presently serving the Lord? All believers are commanded not only to serve but to serve him with gladness (Psalm 100:2). Does gladness describe your service for the King? May this study be just the encouragement you need to "consecrate [your] service unto the Lord" (2 Chronicles 29:5). Are you willing?

Consecrate me now to Thy service Lord,
By the power of grace divine;
Let my soul look up with a steadfast hope,
And my will be lost in Thine.
Fanny Crosby

AMAZING GRACE

*"Take Mark, and bring him with thee: for he is
profitable to me for the ministry." (2 Timothy 4:11)*

Scripture to read: Mark 1:1–45

Have you ever said of someone, "He will never amount to much?"
Or perhaps you've thought, "I'm afraid he'll be nothing but a failure in the ministry." The apostle Paul had similar thoughts about
a young man named John Mark, a resident of Jerusalem. Mark
had a godly mother and was a cousin to Barnabas, a trusted leader
of the early church. This first lesson reveals how Mark became a
dropout and how he was eventually restored as a faithful servant
of the Lord. He was also the human author of this great book,
which bears his name. His story of overcoming the failure of quit-
ting is a comfort and encouragement to us all. Most of us are sincerely grateful that our Lord is willing to give us a second chance
to serve Him.

From the first verse of Mark, we somehow feel he's in a hurry to
tell us the good news of the gospel. He gives a brief introduction
and then begins to reveal wonderful stories of all Jesus did while
walking in Galilee, Samaria, and Judea. He especially shows
us the love and compassion our Servant Lord displayed while

touching, healing, and speaking to poor and needy people. Mark's theme of serving and sacrifice is still a God-honoring pattern for present-day disciples to follow.

Mark is not shy about moving us along from one miracle to another. His favorite word is *straightway*, which means "immediately." Under the direction of the Holy Spirit, he records more of Jesus' deeds than he does of His actual teachings. To the other three Gospel writers he left the writing of Jesus' teaching, ancestry, birth, and childhood.

It's time to buckle on our sandals that we might walk with Mark through this great book. More importantly, it is time to listen and observe the King of servants as He went "about doing good, and healing all that were oppressed of the devil; for God was with Him" (Acts 10:38).

MARK, THE RESTORED SERVANT

Most of our knowledge about Mark is not revealed in the book bearing his name. Details of his life are, instead, given to us in Acts, three of Paul's letters, and 1 Peter.

1. Read Acts 12:12. Who was Mark's mother?

   _____

   What was happening at her home in Jerusalem in this passage?

   _____

   How was Peter delivered from prison, and where did he go after his miraculous deliverance (Acts 12:7–17)?

   _____

John Mark was blessed to have a faithful mother who opened her home to serve members of the early church. Mary was an example of service for Mark and countless other believers, including Peter. Mark's cousin was Barnabas, another prominent servant and encourager in the Jerusalem church. Who are the people in your church who are examples of faithful servants? To whom can you be such an example?

2. When Paul and Barnabas were chosen for their first missionary journey, who accompanied them (Acts 12:25)?

3. This early mission team was only a few weeks into their ministry when John Mark suddenly quit and returned to Jerusalem (Mark 13:13). What possible reasons might have contributed to his departure?

4. Read Acts 15:37–40. On a later mission trip, whom did Barnabas want to include as part of the team?

Who disagreed with this idea?

How was the disagreement settled?

After his desertion from the team, the great apostle Paul dismissed Mark as one not to be trusted in the matter of ministry faithfulness. Paul would not give him a second chance. We are glad, however, for Barnabas, who did. What a difference this great man made in the life of young Mark!

5. According to Paul's later prison letters, Mark had obviously matured in the grace and knowledge of his Lord. Read the following passages and record what Paul wrote about Mark.

• Colossians 4:10

• 2 Timothy 4:11

- Philemon 23–24

From his Roman prison cell, Paul was glad to say that he had been wrong about Mark and that Mark had certainly become a worthy helper. He didn't drag up Mark's past failures but no doubt rejoiced in his obvious growth and usefulness for the work of God. Here we have great humility exhibited by both the godly apostle and his younger helper.

6. Peter, a man who was no stranger to failure himself, also knew and loved Mark. What did he call Mark in 1 Peter 5:13?

7. Read 2 Peter 1:21. How did we get the Word of God?

Mark was one of the men honored to be chosen as one of these writers of Scripture.

8. Read Mark 1:1. This to-the-point author gives us the title of his book in just one sentence. What was it?

In this sentence, how did he also affirm his belief in the deity of Christ?

For the next 677 verses of his book, Mark continued to declare the greatness and mighty works of the Lord he loved. In chapter 1 he takes a few verses to remind us of the ministry of John the Baptist, who declared that the prophecies in the Old Testament regarding a Savior were now fulfilled. John, the humble servant, cried for all who would hear: "Behold the Lamb of God, which taketh away the sin of the world" (John 1:29). Mark also includes Jesus' baptism in the Jordan, when the heavenly Father declared how very pleased He was with His beloved Son.

JESUS CHRIST, THE REDEEMER SERVANT

9. Read Mark 1:14–15. When Jesus began His ministry to sinful mankind, what was His message?

_____

_____

When did you repent and believe the gospel?

_____

The Servant Calls His First Disciples

10. Whom did Jesus call to join Him in ministry (Mark 1:16–17)?

_____

_____

What was He calling them to become?

_____

11. How did the men respond to His call (Mark 1:18–20)?

What did the decision to follow Him cost the new disciples?

_____

Before their call to discipleship, these fishermen had been disciples of John the Baptist. They later met and put their trust in Jesus (John 1:35–42). When called by the Savior as He walked by the Sea of Galilee, their response was immediate. They set aside their own dreams and plans and surrendered all to follow Him. They could never have imagined all this decision would mean and all they would witness as they followed the Lamb of God. They would also discover that fishing for men was much more difficult than fishing for fish!

The Servant Ministers in Capernaum

12. Read Mark 1:21. What was the first thing Jesus did on the Sabbath day in Capernaum?

_____

5

How did His hearers respond to Jesus' teaching (Mark 1:22)?

_____

What do you think Mark meant when he said Jesus taught "as one that had authority, and not as the scribes"?

_____

_____

13. What man in the synagogue was especially interested in the new teacher (Mark 1:23)?

_____

Before this afflicted man could speak, who cried out (Mark 1:23) from inside the man's body? What did this voice say (Mark 1:24)?

_____

_____

14. How did Jesus show His almighty power over the forces of the Evil One (Mark 1:25–26)?

_____

Read Mark 1:27. What effect did this victory over evil have on those who were listening?

_____

Imagine those who stood near in the temple and heard this conversation between the Lord and the demon! This evil one knew well that Jesus was the Holy One of God. This is the fourth statement of Jesus' deity found in the first twenty-four verses of Mark. Note that while devils confessed that Jesus was the Son of God, others present in the synagogue did not.

From the very public miracle in God's house, Mark now brings us to a private Sabbath supper at Peter's house. Undoubtedly the disciples looked forward to an opportunity to discuss with the Master the astonishing events of the day. What a privilege for Peter's family to have the Son of God as their guest! Only our all-knowing Lord was ready for the sad news awaiting them inside Peter's front door.

15. Read Mark 1:30–31. Upon entering the fisherman's home, what serious situation did they discover?

What prayer request did Peter and his family bring to the Great Physician?

How did our Lord respond to Peter's cry for help?

What household responsibilities did the now healthy mother-in-law return to at once?

He touched her hand, and the fever left her,

He touched her hand as only He can,

With the wondrous skill of the Great Physician,

With the tender touch of the Son of Man,

And the lips that had been parched and burning

Trembled with thanks that she could now speak,

And she rose and ministered to her household,

She rose and ministered unto Him.

Serving the Lord is one of the best ways to show thanksgiving for His goodness. Peter's house had gone from being a hospital to a place of hospitality. In her weakness, others had waited on his mother-in law, but soon she was up setting the table and broiling the fish! Do you think Peter's family ever forgot the events of this joyful Sabbath? Over and over they must have told the story of how Jesus took her hand into His almighty hand and healed her completely. What interesting talk they must have had around the supper table that night!

16. Read Mark 1:32–34. As the sun set, the whole city came outside Peter's house! Why had they come?

How did the Great Physician respond to those who were sick with pitiful ailments?

_____

17. Read Mark 1:35. Before Peter's mother-in-law was up and baking the biscuits for breakfast, Who else was already up?

_____

Why was He up so early, and where did He go?

_____

Why do you think Mark included this verse about Jesus spending time alone with His Father?

_____

_____

18. Mark 1:36–39 reveals that His fellowship time was interrupted. Who came looking for Him, and what message did they bring to Jesus?

_____

_____

What new places of ministry did He now announce to His disciples?

_____

Before closing chapter 1, Mark introduces us to a third needy person who was in need of the Great Physician. Long deserted by his family and friends and relegated to die a painful death, this poor man was desperate to meet our loving and sympathizing Lord.

19. Read Mark 1:40–42. What was the man's disease, and what was his statement of faith regarding the power of Jesus?

_____

_____

How did Jesus reward the faith of this man, and how long did it take the leprosy to leave his body?

_____

_____

How long did it take for the leprosy to leave the man's body?

The same mighty hand that lifted up Peter's mother-in-law now reached out without hesitation to a deformed, leprous man. Sadly this man had been untouched since the onset of his loathsome disease. Other lepers had been his only contacts, since healthy people were forbidden to come near those in the leper colonies on the outskirts of town. Now fully cleansed, he could once again return home to his family. Christ had given him new life, and he would never stop talking about the mighty power of the Son of God!

20. Read Mark 1:43–44. Before returning home, there were two things Jesus required of this man. What were they?

Why do you think Jesus commanded him to "say nothing to any man"?

Why was he instructed to show himself to the priest? Read Leviticus 14:1–7.

21. What was the result of the cleansed man not obeying Jesus' first command (Mark 1:45)?

Jesus told this man to keep quiet, and yet he told everybody. Jesus commands us to tell everybody—and we keep quiet![1]

THINK ON THESE THINGS

✝ Mark's life reminds us that our God is One Who is willing to give His children a second chance. We have all grieved our Lord with a thousand falls. From Mark we learn that through repentance and true godly sorrow (2 Corinthians 7:10), we can begin a new life of profitable service for God. If we then accomplish anything for God, we know it is because of the *amazing* grace of our long-suffering God. "By the [*amazing*] grace of God I am what I am" (1 Corinthians 15:10).

✛ Just as He called four fishermen in this lesson, Jesus still calls women to follow Him. How long have you been following the Lord? What have been the joy and sacrifices that serving Him has brought to your life? In Mark 1, the four fishermen observed unbelievable joys. However, they would begin to experience long days with hardly time to eat. They would also come face to face with many who hated the Master. So it will be with us. Will we follow and serve when faced with "dangers, toils, and snares"?

✛ Our praying Master needs praying servants, a truth Peter, Andrew, James, and John learned and all disciples must learn. The record Mark gives us of Jesus rising before dawn to be with His Father is just one of similar examples recorded for us in the Gospels that Jesus longed to be with His Father. When in your day do you take time to be alone with your heavenly Father? Here is an important truth I'm still trying to learn: *The time we spend with God is more important than the work we do for God.*

✛ It is good to remember all the people in Mark 1 who were served by the Lord. Think of those He touched and of the compassion He showed for suffering men and women. From the wilderness to the seaside, from God's house to Peter's house; from His early solitary place to the desert places of verse 45, He sought to serve. As we end this first lesson, let us ask who we can serve today in the name of our Lord.

> *Jesus Master, Whom I serve,*
> *Though so feebly and so ill,*
> *Strengthen hand and heart and nerve,*
> *All Thy bidding to fulfill.*
> *Open Thou mine eyes to see,*
> *All the work Thou hast for me.*
> *Frances R. Havergal*

SHADOW SERVANTS

Those Who Served the Master and His Disciples

Each of these lessons from Mark includes the lives of faithful men and women who happily served God in the shadow of well-known servants of the Lord. Many of their names have long been forgotten, or were never recorded at all. Together with well-known servants, they served "under the shadow of the Almighty" (Psalm 91:1).

The first two lessons will include those who served our Lord and His disciples, as well as those who served in the shadow of the apostle Paul. Future lessons will reveal shadow servants who served in the ministries of Charles Spurgeon, Hudson Taylor, George Muller, and others.

Our first shadow servants are found in the pages of the Gospels. One of these unnamed women we met in this lesson. We know her only by her connection to the apostle Peter; she was his mother-in-law. Unable to serve anyone due to a raging fever, she rejoiced when the Master took her fevered hand and lifted her up to perfect health. She was then glad to serve supper to Him and His disciples! Certainly she served her Lord many other times when He lodged at Peter's home.

In Luke 8:2–3, we are introduced to "certain women" who also followed Jesus and served Him in the shadows as He went about doing good. Some of these women had been delivered of evil spirits as well as other various illnesses. Included in this group was Mary Magdalene, who was delivered from seven wicked demons. Joanna, whose husband worked for King Herod, was also one who served in the shadows. A woman named Susanna is also named, although no information is included about her.

Luke mentioned "many others" who ministered to Jesus "of their substance." These women owed a tremendous debt to the Lord and were glad to use their time and money to follow Him and the disciples as they traveled. What are some of the ways they might have ministered to Him and the throngs of people who followed Him everywhere He went? Did this group of women leave all to follow the Savior as the disciples had done? Some were financially able to travel around Galilee, Samaria, and Judea. We should give thanks for their generous hearts and for their love for the Master. We should also be sincerely envious of all they saw, heard, and experienced as they walked with the Lord.

Some of these same women were also part of the group we read of in Matthew 27:55–56. There were "many women" at Calvary "beholding afar off" all that happened on the day the Lord died on the cross. Along with Mary, the mother of Jesus, a few of the group are named, including the mother (Salome) of disciples James and John. These had faithfully followed Him from Galilee, "ministering unto Him." In three days some gladly greeted the dawn, as they looked for ways to show their love by arriving early to the tomb to care for His body. Some of them even talked with an angel that morning and rejoiced to hear that the crucified Lord was not in the tomb. He wasn't there because He had risen from the dead! After the angel showed them the place where He had lain, they believed and then left quickly to tell the disciples the good news.

It is interesting to note that the disciples, with the exception of John, were not at Calvary. They were also absent from the garden tomb on that morning. It was this faithful group of women shadow servants who grieved over the death of their Lord and then rejoiced to tell of His resurrection.

I am glad to honor these godly shadow servants. They heard the Master call and then left all to "minister unto him of their substance" (Luke 8:2–3). Shadow servants are still needed today! I give thanks for many of you who are working in the shadows at your church, Christian school, camp ministry, hospitals and nursing homes, or with faithful missionaries in faraway places. May you continue to be "stedfast, unmovable, always abounding in the work of the Lord, forasmuch as ye know that your labor is not in vain in the Lord " (1 Corinthians 15:58).

JESUS, WHAT A FRIEND FOR SINNERS!

*"I came not to call the righteous, but sinners to
repentance." (Mark 2:17)*

Scripture to read: Mark 2:1–3:19

Our second lesson from Mark's Gospel brings us again to the
seaside village of Capernaum. This small village witnessed some
of Jesus' greatest miracles. We will visit two homes in Capernaum
and take a walk through a nearby cornfield on the Sabbath as we
make our way to the town synagogue. In the midst of all this activity, two men will have their bodies, and their hearts, restored by
Jesus.

As he weaves together the great events of this portion of Scripture,
Mark reveals to us the heart responses of those close to the Master.
Of course, we will see the compassionate heart of Jesus on display.
But we will also see hearts of faith, hardened hearts of unbelief,
curious hearts, as well as obedient hearts. We will notice that some
hearts gladly heard His preaching and followed Him, while other
hearts carped and criticized Him at every turn. Such withered
hearts denied His deity, even while observing His miracles of healing stricken and frail bodies. Their hearts became so wicked they

were even willing to join with their enemies to destroy the friend of sinners.

As we read the responses from the people in Capernaum, we need to remember that the men and women in our present century have the very same responses to Christ that these residents had centuries ago. Every human heart is still "deceitful above all things, and desperately wicked" (Jeremiah 17:9). Jesus has commanded present-day disciples to "keep [their hearts] with all diligence" (Proverbs 4:23). He has also commanded us to show needy people around us that He not only is the friend of sinners but also the lover of their souls.

HEARTS OF FAITH

1. Read Mark 2:1–2 and then describe the scene Jesus saw when He entered the packed house at Capernaum.

    _____

    _____

    Notice the last words of verse 2. How did Jesus seek to minister to the overflow crowd?

    _____

    What might have been His message? See Mark 1:15 for a clue.

    _____

    _____

2. What unusual activity interrupted His preaching (Mark 2:3–4)?

    _____

    What was the reason for this interruption?

    _____

3. This poor helpless man had both a spiritual and a physical need. Which did Jesus deal with first (Mark 2:5)?

    _____

4.   How did this paralyzed man and his friends demonstrate faith?

_____

Forgiveness of sin is God's greatest gift to us because it meets man's greatest need. The Lord rewarded the faith of these five men by healing the man's soul as well as his paralyzed body.

HEARTS OF UNBELIEF

5.   While Jesus saw the faith of the men on the roof, what did He also see in the hearts of certain scribes who were present in the packed house (Mark 2:6–8)?

_____   _____

_____

What were these religious unbelievers thinking about Jesus?

_____   _____

6.   How did Jesus respond to their blasphemous thoughts (Mark 2:8–11)?

_____

Read Mark 2:12. How did the sick man respond to Jesus' command?

_____

How did the people crowded into the house respond (Mark 2:12)?

_____

The Lord's enemies could deny Jesus' power to forgive sin, but they couldn't deny His power to heal. The proof was standing in front of them! Once helpless and without hope, this one who had entered the house via the roof now miraculously exited the place by walking through the door! This happy scene caused a preacher in Belfast, Northern Ireland to exclaim:

> Here is a man who, when he came to the Lord Jesus, had his head on the bed. But when he left, he had the bed on his head. Now that was a miracle that raised the roof![1]

A HEART OF COMPASSION

Followed by the crowds as He walked along the seaside, Jesus continued to instruct needy people regarding repentance and belief in the good news of the gospel. On this walk, however, He intentionally passed by the local tax office. Here He called another of His disciples to follow Him. What an unusual place to find a disciple! Jesus, Who knows the hearts of all men, knew one taxman whose heart was prepared to begin a new career!

7. Read Mark 2:14. What were Jesus' first words to Levi (Matthew)?

_____

What was the tax collector's immediate response?

_____

8. In Mark 2:15 Jesus was in yet another Capernaum home, this one not quite as crowded as the earlier house with the broken roof. Whose house was now privileged to have Jesus as a guest? Who were the other invited guests?

_____

_____

Matthew, the new convert, "arranged to bring all of his old friends to meet all of his new friends!"[2] He began his new life by introducing fellow tax collectors to Jesus. Think of hated tax collectors breaking bread with such well-known Jewish fishermen as Peter, Andrew, and the Zebedee brothers. Publicans, or tax collectors, were Jews like Matthew who had chosen to collect taxes for the hated Roman government. They did not follow the Jewish law or take interest in religion. All true Jews regarded them to be money-greedy cheats and traitors to the Jewish faith—just the kind of people Jesus came to call to repentance!

9. What do you think Jesus showed to these publicans and sinners that their religious leaders had never shown?

_____

What do you think Jesus' message was to them (see Mark 1:15)?

_____

In Matthew's Gospel we read that Jesus was a "friend of publicans and sinners" (11:19). As he wrote these words later, Matthew must have remembered the day Jesus joined him in breaking bread with needy publicans and sinners. He would never forget the heart of compassion on display as the Master preached the word of salvation to sinners. Jesus' preaching at Matthew's house, with his friends willingly listening, was as great a miracle as the healing at the house with the hole in the roof. Do you remember the day He showed you His pity, love, and power? Give Him thanks!

> *Come ye sinners, poor and needy,*
> *Weak and wounded, sick and sore;*
> *Jesus ready stands to save you,*
> *Full of pity, love, and power.*
> *I will arise and go to Jesus,*
> *He will embrace me in His arms;*
> *In the arms of my dear Savior,*
> *O there are ten thousand charms.*
> *Joseph Hart*

10. What was the response of the self-righteous scribes and Pharisees when they saw Jesus eating at Matthew's house (Mark 2:16)?

_____

Read Mark 2:17–22. How did Jesus respond to their criticism, and what do you think He meant?

_____

HARDENED HEARTS

11. On His way to the synagogue in Capernaum, Jesus and His disciples walked through a garden. Mark 2:23 says the disciples were hungry and decided to have a snack. What food did they enjoy?

_____

Who observed this "illegal" Sabbath activity and quickly attacked the Lord (Mark 2:24)?

_____

12. Read Mark 2:25–26. What portion of God's Word did Jesus use to answer His enemies?

_____

_____

God had created the Sabbath to be a weekly blessing to the Jewish people. Because the religious leaders of Jesus' day had added countless man-made rules and regulations to God's original commandments, the Sabbath had ceased to be a blessing but instead had become a tremendous burden. Attempting to keep all the rules made the Sabbath anything but a day of rest.

Jesus' activities on the Sabbath greatly offended the self-righteous keepers of the law. In their minds, Jesus and His disciples were offenders of all that was sacred, and they were not bashful about confronting Him. Jesus was always quick to answer their false charges, using a portion of the Word to support His answers. He was not afraid to openly defy the authority claimed by the hypocrites before Him.

13. What two closing statements regarding the Sabbath did Jesus use to silence His enemies (Mark 2:27–28)?

_____

_____

14. Read Mark 3:1–5. To show He was indeed Lord of the Sabbath, what wonderful miracle did Jesus perform in the synagogue?

_____

_____

With this miracle, what helpful truths was He teaching the people about the Sabbath (Mark 3:4)?

_____

_____

15. Mark 3:5 records that Jesus was angry with the Pharisees. Why was He angry?

_____

When the Pharisees left the synagogue, what heinous crime did they plan (Mark 3:6)?

_____

These men felt breaking the Sabbath was a horrendous offense while the crime of murder was fully acceptable to them!

CURIOUS HEARTS

While Jesus' enemies plotted to destroy the One Who came down from the Father, countless others enthusiastically sought to be near Him. Mark makes it clear, however, that most of these clamored only to see His miracles, not to hear His message.

16. Read Mark 3:7–8. The "great multitude" surrounding Jesus had heard of His mighty deeds and had come from every corner of the country. Where specifically had these curious followers come from?

_____

_____

17. How does Mark say the Lord responded to the countless diseased and tortured people that sought His help (Mark 3:10)?

_____

According to Mark 3:11, what testimony, denied by the Pharisees, did the unclean spirits believe?

_____

OBEDIENT HEARTS

From the throngs of men who followed Jesus, He called only twelve to be His disciples. He called and they came. The greatest test of disciples is a willingness to follow their master. These twelve were certainly not mighty men of faith, wealth, or abilities. They were "weak things" who would one day "confound the things which are mighty" (1 Corinthians 1:27). Having such unlikely candidates in Jesus' training school is a great encouragement to us. We should be glad He still calls weak thing to do His work.

18. Read Mark 3:14–15. Jesus required His apostles to do two things. What were they?

_____

_____

Notice which of these Jesus mentioned first. From the beginning, Jesus taught His disciples that they must not overlook the necessity of spending time with Him. If they did so, they would have no power to carry out their ministry. The apostle John recorded these words of Jesus: "Without me ye can do nothing" (John 15:5). This is the same truth Jesus still requires of every servant who would follow Him.

19. Earlier Mark introduced us to five of the disciples. What are the names of the group of twelve (Mark 3:16–19)?

_____

_____

_____

Whose name is listed first? Whose name is listed last?

_____

At least two other places in the Gospels list all the apostles. Peter is always listed first, followed by the names of the other Galilean fishermen. Judas is always listed last, followed by the somber testimony of his betrayal of the Master.

THINK ON THESE THINGS

✝ The people of Capernaum saw many of Jesus' mightiest works. They were often amazed and astonished at all they saw and heard. Matthew, who was from Capernaum, recorded in 11:23–24, however, that the residents continued to walk in great unbelief and rejection of Jesus' message. How sad that this privileged town would one day hear Jesus say they would be accountable for taking so lightly all they had seen and heard. Will we not also be accountable for taking lightly, or ignoring, the great opportunities God has given us to fellowship with Him and to give out His message? "For unto whomsoever much is given, of him shall be much required" (Luke 12:48).

✢ There were four unnamed men in this lesson who were determined to bring their friend to Jesus. They knew if they could get him to the Master, his life would be changed forever.

> Someone suggested we call them, Frank Faith, Larry Love, Harry Hope and Gary Grit. These men epitomized all these attributes. They were not only prepared to take the man to Jesus but to use innovative means to do so.[3]

✢ While most of the crowds who sought to be with Jesus did not really want to leave all and follow Him, we should be thankful for the twelve men who said yes when He called. They were weak and untaught, but Jesus saw their hearts and He desired their fellowship as He walked throughout the land of the Jews inviting sinners to come to Him for eternal life. Are we willing to be His servant and follow Him fully? When He looks at our heart, does He see full surrender?

> *O lead me, Lord, that I may lead*
> *The wandering and the wavering feet;*
> *O feed me, Lord, that I may feed*
> *Thy hungering ones with manna sweet.*
> *O use me, Lord, use even me,*
> *Just as Thou wilt, and when, and where,*
> *Until Thy blessed face I see,*
> *Thy rest, Thy joy, Thy glory share.*
> *Frances R. Havergal*

SHADOW SERVANTS

Those Who Served with Paul

Throughout Paul's epistles he sprinkles numerous names of shadow servants whose joy was to serve with him "under the shadow of the Almighty" (Psalm 91:1). The largest concentration of these people is found in Romans 16, and it is these godly men and women we honor in this lesson.

Under the inspiration of the Holy Spirit, Paul wrote the mighty book of Romans while in the city of Corinth. In the opening verses of the book, he announced to whom he was writing: "To all that be in Rome, beloved of God, called to be saints" (1:7). Have you ever wondered who made up this ordinary group of saints? Before closing his letter, Paul introduced us to about thirty of these Greek, Roman, and Jewish shadow servants.

Paul had never been to Rome, but in his busy ministry he had either crossed paths with these men and women or heard their testimonies from other believers. No doubt he had introduced many of them to the Lord Jesus Christ. Certainly he instructed and encouraged them to be busy serving God wherever they had opportunity. God brought this group together in the historical city of Rome. There they sought out other believers and became a part of the church to whom Paul was writing.

In the first two verses of Romans 16, we are introduced to Sister Phoebe, who lived near Corinth. Paul said she was a "servant of the church," and she was probably a businesswoman. She was soon to embark on a long and tiring journey to Rome, and Paul asked her to carry the mighty letter he had written to his beloved friends. Phoebe could never have imagined that the contents of the letter she carried would spark the Reformation in Europe centuries after she and Paul rested from their labors. What care this reliable servant must have taken to ensure its safety as she traveled by land and sea to Rome.

Receiving Phoebe at the end of her journey were the saints Paul addressed in Romans 16:3–16. Certainly Priscilla and Aquila welcomed her and were eager to hear any news from their dear friend Paul. This godly couple, no doubt, made Phoebe feel right at home and introduced her to the members of the church who were meeting in their house.

As you read through the list of names in these verses, note how Paul wrote encouraging and loving comments for his fellow laborers. Some in the list may have been well-to-do; others were probably slaves or servants to the wealthy and powerful of Rome. Some had served in prison with Paul; some had first heard of Jesus as Paul preached. Perhaps as many as nine were faithful women. All were ordinary people willing to "present their bodies a living sacrifice, holy, acceptable unto God," considering this to be their "reasonable service" (Romans 12:1–2).

It was this little group of servants who first heard the beloved words of the book of Romans. Imagine having such an honor! Certainly the portion of the epistle that we know as 8:28–39 brought great comfort to their hearts. About six years after he wrote Romans, Paul and many of those listed in chapter 16 were persecuted or put to death because they loved and preached Christ.

Until we meet them in heaven, we won't know their life and death stories. But I am so grateful that the Holy Spirit directed Paul to include their names for our encouragement and blessing. It is no wonder that their faith was, and continues to be, spoken of throughout the whole world (Romans 1:8). How Paul loved these shadow servants who served together with him "under the shadow of the Almighty" (Psalm 91:1)!

Lesson 3
SCATTERING PRECIOUS SEED

"Behold, there went out a sower to sow." (Mark 4:3)

Scripture to read: Mark 3:20–4:34

The prophet Isaiah, speaking of Christ, foretold that He would be "despised and rejected of men, a man of sorrows, and acquainted with grief" (53:3). The events of this lesson take place early in the Lord's ministry, yet the opposition and rejection were already strong against Him. Not only did the religious leaders hate and oppose Him but also His mother, Mary, and His earthly brothers and sisters attempted to hinder His ministry.

Mark reminds us of the multitudes who thronged the Master everywhere He went. In the Scriptures for this lesson, Jesus performed no miracles. His emphasis, instead, was on teaching the truths of the kingdom. Sadly, most of the multitudes had ears, but they would not hear or understand the precious seeds of truth He scattered throughout Galilee. They were thrilled to see His mighty miracles, but most rejected His message of faith and repentance.

We read in Mark 4:2 that "he taught them many things." May He also teach us many things as we study this portion of Mark. Unlike the multitudes, however, may we have ears that hear and obey all the Lord says to us. And may we, like Jesus, be about the business of faithfully scattering the precious seeds of the gospel to the souls He sends across our path.

THE MASTER MISUNDERSTOOD

1. Read Mark 3:20. Mark tells us multitudes of people gathered everywhere Jesus and the disciples went. This constant presence of the crowd interrupted what important part of their daily schedule?

_____

In Mark 3:21, what group expressed opposition to Jesus? What was their hurtful charge against Him?

_____

We can only imagine the talk around the tables in Nazareth as Jesus' friends and kinsmen met to discuss His well-known works and words. We expect to read of opposition from the self-righteous religious leaders, but these charges from His friends and family must have surely grieved His heart.

THE MASTER OPPOSED BY HIS ENEMIES

Local scribes and Pharisees had dogged Jesus from the beginning of His ministry (Mark 2:6, 16; 3:2–6). Unable to stem His growing popularity, they had sent to Jerusalem for more educated and experienced temple teachers to discredit Jesus the law breaker. Reinforcements soon arrived. After completing their seventy-five-mile journey to Galilee, these hypocrites wasted no time in making their most vicious attack yet against the Master.

2. What was their shameful accusation against Jesus (Mark 3:22)?

_____

Unable to deny that Jesus had done great miracles, they accused Him of doing His works in partnership with the Devil! His ministry was being done through satanic power, not the power of God.

3. Read Mark 3:23–26. After calling His accusers to come closer, with what question did Jesus answer their accusations?

_____

4. What examples did He use to demonstrate the foolishness of their accusations (Mark 3:23–26)?

_____

Jesus had come to earth to destroy the works of the Wicked One (1 John 3:8). How absurd that Satan would join forces with the Master to destroy his own kingdom! Mortal men are powerless against Satan, but the Lord, the Mighty Conqueror, will one day destroy forever Satan and his demons (Revelation 20:2–3, 10).

> *The prince of darkness grim,*
> *We tremble not for Him,*
> *His rage we can endure,*
> *For lo, his doom is sure;*
> *One little word shall fell him.*
> *Martin Luther*

5. Mark 3:28–30 is a solemn passage. What does Jesus say about sin and forgiveness in 3:28?

_____

Perhaps the apostle John was thinking of this incident later when he wrote the comforting words of 1 John 1:7, 9 that Jesus will forgive all our sins if we confess them.

6. What do you think Mark 3:29 means?

_____

_____

Some Bible commentators believe the scribes had committed this very sin by attributing to Satan miracles Jesus had performed. They knew His miracles were not satanic but the work of God. Nevertheless, their black hearts deliberately declared His works to be those of the Devil. These scribes were indeed in danger of eternal damnation for such blasphemous statements.

Another commentator says this about "the unpardonable sin."

> Multitudes have tortured themselves with the thought that they have committed some act of sin that has placed them beyond the reach of Divine forgiveness. This passage does not speak of any act of sin as unpardonable. A man may so harden himself in sin as to become incapable of repenting, and because he cannot repent, he cannot be forgiven. Does a man ever get into this awful state? I cannot tell; but those who mourn because they think they have committed this sin prove by their very brokenheartedness that they have not committed it.[1]

THE MASTER OPPOSED BY HIS FAMILY

7.   In Mark 3:31, who sought an opportunity to visit with Jesus?

In Mark 6:3 we are told the names of some of Jesus' family members. Who are they?

What does John tell us about these family members (John 7:5)?

8.   Read Psalm 69:8. Centuries earlier, what had David prophesied about Jesus and His earthly family?

Undoubtedly Mary, James, Joses, Jude, Simon, and His sisters had heard of Jesus' growing fame. Perhaps they had come to Capernaum to rescue Him from such a busy life and had sought to take Him back to the quiet little town of Nazareth. But the crowd was so great that the only way they could get His attention was to send a messenger to announce their desire to see Him. We find His answer to them in Mark 3:33–35.

9. Do you think Jesus was renouncing His family or being unkind to them when He asked the rhetorical question in 3:33? What do you think He meant?

_____

Jesus loved His family even more than they loved Him. His purpose here was to teach that He invites the entire world into His intimate and divine family. Even being a member of Jesus' own earthly family did not merit salvation by virtue of that relationship. His natural mother, half brothers, and half sisters needed to be saved from sin. "All of those, and only those, who believe in Me are spiritually related to Me," He was saying.[2]

10. What does Jesus require of those who would be members of His family (Mark 3:35)?

_____

11. Throughout Scripture sinful man is invited to come to Jesus if he would have eternal life. What invitations are found in the following verses:

• Isaiah 55:1–3

_____

• Matthew 11:28–29

_____

• John 7:37

_____

• Revelation 22:17

_____

When did you accept God's loving invitation and become a member of His family?

Jesus' human family were not all members of His spiritual family at this time. Later, some of them did trust His shed blood as payment for their sins (Acts 1:14). His brothers James and Jude were chosen to author New Testament books bearing their names.

We aren't told if all Mary and Joseph's children believed on Jesus. What a tragedy for them to share an earthly home with Him but reject His gift of an eternal home. What a tragedy, also, for anyone who reads and studies this book of Mark and then chooses to reject His salvation.

THE MASTER TELLS A STORY

In John 7:46, one of Jesus' disciples wrote of Him, "Never man spake like this man." John was, no doubt, present by the seaside when the Master first spoke the words recorded for us in chapter 4. I hope Jesus' mother and His half brothers stayed around to hear this important story about seeds and soil.

12. Read Mark 4:1. Describe Jesus' classroom and the number of His students.

   According to Mark 4:2, what teaching method did He use to impart His truths?

In the Gospels, Jesus used more than thirty parables in His teaching. This parable of the sower is one of the most well-known, and it is the only one we will deal with in this lesson.

In the Bible, a parable is a short, simple story designed *to reveal* spiritual truth to those who are heavenly minded. Parables were also used by Jesus *to conceal* truth from those whose minds were only on the things of this world.

13. Read Mark 4:3–9 and describe the four types of soil Jesus mentioned in the parable.

   What do you think the seed represents? The sower?

What happened to the seeds that were sown by the sower?

_____

14. What important command did Jesus give to the great crowd when He finished His story (Mark 4:9)?

_____   _____

_____

Most of the people in this great crowd were blind to spiritual truth. Because of this, Jesus left the interpretation of the story up to each hearer. This was not a story just about seeds and soil. That day by the seaside every hearer heard eternal truth that deserved serious attention. Sadly, most in the multitude went away without caring to understand the message of the Master.

15. Who asked Jesus to explain the parable (Mark 4:10)?

_____

16. According to Jesus, what seed was the sower sowing (Mark 4:14)?

_____

17. Read Mark 4:15–20. The hearts of the Capernaum crowd represented the soil Jesus spoke of. Listed below are the four types of human hearts (soil) present that day. How did each one respond to the seed that was sowed?

    • Wayside path soil (verse 15)

    _____

    • Stony soil (verse 16)

    _____

    • Thorny soil (verse 18)

    _____

    • Good soil (verse 20)

    _____

    What hindrances kept most of the seed from producing fruit?

    _____   _____

Which of these soils best matches your own present spiritual condition?

As with the entire Bible, this parable is up-to-date. The seed is still just as powerful as ever (Hebrews 4:12), and present-day hearts respond in the same ways Jesus taught in this story. This is what goes on in all preaching services, Sunday school classes, and youth groups week after week. In each gathering some or all of the hearts pictured here are present. The Devil is still stealing away the seed of the Word, thereby preventing it from taking root in the hearts of hearers. How Satan hates the Word of God!

18. Read Mark 4:23–25. What warnings did Jesus give regarding our ears?

A believer with a spiritual hearing problem is in great danger! What important truth and warning does the psalmist have for the saints in Psalm 85:8?

> *Open my ears, that I may hear*
> *Voices of truth Thou sendest clear,*
> *And while the Scriptures fall on my ear,*
> *Everything false will disappear.*
> *Clara H. Scott*

19. How do you prepare your heart to hear, understand, and obey the preaching and teaching of God's Word?

---

20. Jesus is our example of One Who was always sowing the seed of the Word. Where are you presently sowing precious seed?

Sowing seed is hard work. It calls for faith in the giver of the seed and the seed itself.

21. In the verses below, what promises are given to encourage seed sowers?

    • Psalm 126:6

    _____

    • Isaiah 55:11

    _____

22. All gardeners know that seeds must be watered, which is true of spiritual seed as well. In what ways can we water the seed of the Word that we, or others, have sown?

    • Luke 18:1

    _____

    • John 15:4–5

    _____

    • Hebrews 4:16

    _____

23. Read 1 Corinthians 3:5–9. The work of sowing seed often involves several individuals. In this passage, what part did Paul say he played? What part did his friend Apollos play?

    _____

    In verse 7, what did Paul say about himself and Apollos?

    _____

    What role does God alone play in the process of sowing and watering seed?

    _____

THINK ON THESE THINGS

✝ While on this earth, the Lord was hated by His enemies and sadly misunderstood by His family and friends. Shall we expect anything less? If a woman devotes her life to a noble cause, the world applauds her. But, if she gives herself in total dedication to love and serve God, the world brands her a fanatic. Remember what Jesus' friends and family said about Him: "He is beside himself" (Mark 3:21)! Our friends and family may say the same of us.

✠ The Wicked One is more continually active among good Bible-preaching congregations than almost any other place. From him come wandering thoughts and roving imaginations, drowsy minds, dull ears, sleepy eyes, and distracted attentions. The Devil is present every week in our churches. He never stays away but does his best to immediately steal away any seed sown in our hearts by preachers and teachers. How we need to faithfully pray that our mighty God will bind the Wicked One so that he is unable to steal these precious seeds.

✠ Over one hundred years ago a midwesterner by the name of William Ogden was evidently touched by the great truths found in the parable of the sower. He wrote a hymn about the need of scattering precious seeds wherever we find opportunity. What opportunities do you take to scatter the seed of the gospel? Besides a personal testimony or words of encouragement, I find the use of gospel tracts to be a great way to sow seeds. Always carry tracts with you, asking God to prepare hearts to receive the gospel truth found in each tract. Also remember to water the tracts with faithful prayer.

> *Scattering precious seed, doubting never,*
> *Scattering precious seed, trusting ever;*
> *Sowing the word with prayer and endeavor,*
> *Trusting the Lord for growth and for yield.*
> *William A. Ogden*

SHADOW SERVANTS

Those Who Served with Charles H. Spurgeon— Lavinia Bartlett

In the years that Queen Victoria reigned, Pastor Charles H. Spurgeon was a giant for God in England. However, even a godly giant could not accomplish by himself the great works Spurgeon did for the glory of God. In his shadow, countless men and women served the Lord at the great Metropolitan Tabernacle in London. In our series on shadow servants, we will consider the stories of several of these faithful men and women. In this lesson we will learn about Spurgeon's ladies' Bible study teacher, Mrs. Lavinia Bartlett.

Beginning life in 1806 as Lavinia Hartnell in the Hampshire area of England, Lavinia began what would be a lifelong teaching ministry. Her first students were her siblings, and she carefully passed on to them the Bible knowledge she gained from attending a nearby nonconformist chapel. Eventually she became a Sunday school teacher at the chapel and was known to her students as the "preaching, praying, teacher." For sixteen years she also taught young girls in a boarding school she organized and ran. God was preparing her for a future teaching ministry this simple country girl could not have imagined.

At the age of thirty she married and became Mrs. Bartlett. Because of her new husband's work, they moved to London. Lavinia's health did not do well in such a crowded, damp, and smoky city. She developed a confining heart and lung ailment. Her marriage of seventeen years ended with the sudden death of her husband from cholera.

Lavinia had been blessed with two sons, Edward and George. Their spiritual training, she felt, was her most important teaching opportunity. She went about it with much prayer and faithfulness.

Meanwhile, in another area of London, a very young preacher who was not much older than Lavinia's sons was causing great interest. Charles Spurgeon, at the age of twenty, was called to pastor the New Park Street Chapel. News of the country boy preacher reached Lavinia's sons, and they soon joined the crushing crowds that gladly heard him preach. Soon both Bartlett boys were saved and baptized at the chapel.

As for Lavinia, she would have nothing to do with the "boy wonder." Feeling he was a passing fad, she resisted invitations from her sons to join them at the chapel. Eventually she could resist the invitations no longer. Once she sat under Spurgeon's preaching, she would go nowhere else. At the age of fifty she happily joined her sons as a member of what would eventually become Metropolitan Tabernacle in South London.

It was soon after she joined the famous church that Deacon Thomas Olney encouraged Lavinia to teach a ladies' Bible class. She accepted, and the class came to be known throughout Britain as "Mrs. Bartlett's Class." For sixteen years God greatly used this humble shadow servant to teach hundreds of women. At its height, the class numbered eight hundred. Humanly speaking one wonders how a frail little woman had the strength to teach so many while unaided by a sound system! One can almost hear her pleading voice as she used her very familiar challenge to the women: "Keep near the Cross, my sisters!"

Her pastor spoke often of her value. "He regarded Mrs. Bartlett as his right-hand supporter in Christian labor, and never thought of her without the deepest gratitude to God for raising up so zealous a co-worker."[3] He publicly stated that over eight hundred women had become members of his church through the ministry of Mrs. Bartlett. What gospel seeds she sowed throughout London! She also watered those seeds with faithful prayer and visits to women in the slums as well as to women in upper society.

Upon her death in 1875, her beloved pastor led the church family in grieving the loss of one of his most faithful shadow servants. He preached her funeral before thousands at the tabernacle. A great throng of her sorrowing class members, along with her church friends, were present as her body was laid to rest on Dissenter's Row, Nunhead Cemetery, South London.

The grieving women of her Bible class gave the money to erect a special pink granite monument in her honor. The inscription on the monument was written by Pastor Spurgeon, who made sure he included Lavinia's well-known admonition to her women, "Keep near the Cross, my sisters!" That is still a good admonition for us all, isn't it?

TELL ME THE STORIES OF JESUS

"Such mighty works are wrought by his hands."
(Mark 6:2)

Scripture to read: Mark 4:35–6:6

The four stories of Jesus found in this portion of Mark are ones I always love to hear! What powerful action Mark records, not just for our enjoyment but for our spiritual growth.

The passages considered here begin and end with tragic examples of unbelief. In between we discover fear, a mighty storm, no faith, a pillow, a graveyard, and multitudes of people and pigs! In addition, there are broken chains, thousands of demons, a mass drowning, a new evangelist, a twelve-year-old girl, a woman incurably ill for twelve years, believing faith, laughing scorn, and at least eleven important questions.

Perhaps the saddest people in these stories are those who asked Jesus to leave them alone! The Gadarenes and the Nazarenes had no need of the Lord of glory; therefore, He left them to their sin of unbelief. They rejected the ruler of all nature, and refused "to retain God in their knowledge" (Romans 1:28). Like countless sinners throughout the ages, they professed themselves to be so wise that they didn't need God. Sadly, they rejected the wisdom of God and became fools for all eternity (Romans 1:22).

POWER OVER CREATION

1. Read Mark 4:35–38. After Jesus taught the multitudes by the seaside, what instructions did He give to the disciples?

_____

_____

While in the path of duty, they were suddenly faced with what unexpected event?

_____

To whom did the panic-stricken disciples turn for help? Of what did they accuse Jesus?

_____

Why do you think Jesus was asleep in the back of the ship?

_____

How could being asleep have been a part of the Master's plan to mature His disciples? Read 1 Peter 1:7 for help with your answer.

_____

When storms arise in the life of a believer, he too can cry out for help. His cry will be heard by the Lord of creation, and He will not fail to rise up with help in the time of trouble (Psalm 46:1).

2. What does Mark 4:39, 41 reveal about the power of the Master?

_____

The weary Savior asleep on a borrowed pillow is a picture of His humanity. He knew He was greater than the storm and that it was not time for Him to die, so He slept on. The mighty Savior, standing to rebuke the raging wind and sea, pictures for us His deity. Because He was fully God, and man, He fully understands the trials and infirmities we experience. He has felt them, and He is the very Savior we weary humans require every day of our pilgrim journey.

3. After rebuking the wind and speaking to the sea, whom else did Jesus rebuke (Mark 4:40)?

_____

What was the reason for this rebuke, and what two questions in verse 40 did the Master ask the disciples?

_____

_____

_____

How would others describe your faith? How would your pastor describe it?

_____

_____

The twelve disciples had heard Jesus' sermons. They had seen Him perform mighty miracles, yet they had no faith in Him. Their sin of unbelief caused them to doubt the Master's care for them.

Why did you fear? Why don't you have any faith? Why could you not trust Me? These are the same questions He asks of us all.[1]

A truth for disciples to remember: Little faith is not a little sin!

4. Both Mark 4:38 and 4:41 mention the disciples' having fear. What was the difference between these two types of fear? Read Proverbs 1:7 for help with your answer.

_____

_____

POWER OVER DEMONS

As wonderful as was the story of the calming of the storm, the scene that greeted Jesus and the disciples when they arrived in the country of the Gadarenes is still more amazing! They had passed through a stormy night, and as they stepped on shore they faced an even stormier day. This compelling story began on a hillside when they were approached by a resident of the cemetery who was very much alive.

5.   Read Mark 5:1–5 and answer these questions. After Jesus' ship docked, who immediately approached the Savior?

_____

Describe the dwelling place and the daily life of this poor man.

_____

_____

Why was he in such a miserable condition?

_____

This pitiful man had a cruel and wicked taskmaster—Satan. One author said he was the Devil's prize exhibit, horribly tormented and driven day and night by the vast number of demons dwelling in him.

What a sight he must have been! What ruin sin makes of man. His state is the same that the enemy of our souls would inflict on us all if only he had the power. In this story, Christ's complete authority over the Devil and his demons should be an encouragement to us all.

6.   When the man saw Jesus, what was his first response (Mark 5:6–7)?

_____

Who was actually speaking to Jesus through the man (Mark 5:7)?

_____

What did they acknowledge about the Savior, and of what did they accuse Him (Mark 5:7–9)?

_____

_____

7. Read Mark 5:8. What mighty command did Jesus speak to the tormentors?

_____

What question did He ask the demons, and what was their answer (Mark 5:9)?

_____

_____

The man of Gadara was controlled by a legion—or thousands—of unclean spirits. These cruel, malicious beings were no match for the loving and compassionate Savior. One mightier than the destroyer was on the scene, and the evidence of His omnipotent power was now "sitting and clothed, and in his right mind" (Mark 5:15). As one preacher observed, the resident of the graveyard was now a resident of the "grace-yard!"

> *Wonderful grace of Jesus,*
> *Reaching the most defiled,*
> *By its transforming power,*
> *Making him God's dear child!*
> *Haldor Lillenas*

8. After reading Mark 5:10–13, answer these questions. What request did the evil spirits ask of Jesus?

_____

What was Jesus' response?

_____

How did the two thousand demon-possessed pigs respond to their new residents (Mark 5:13)?

_____

9. Read Mark 5:14–17. As soon as the pigs were in their watery grave, their caretakers fled from the scene. Where did they go, and who accompanied them back to stand before Jesus?

_____

_____

The last words of verse 15 state that these men who saw the former demoniac were afraid. Why do you think they were fearful?

_____

_____

Why did none of the people on the hillside rejoice over the deliverance of this poor man?

_____

Why do you think the owners and keepers of the pigs wanted Jesus to leave Gadara?

_____

10. There was at least one Gadarene on the hillside who grieved because Jesus was leaving. What request did this grateful man make of his new Lord and Master (Mark 5:18)?

_____

Jesus not only delivered this man, He gave him a new mission in life. Instead of following the Master back to Capernaum, where was the new evangelist to go (Mark 5:19)?

_____

11. What message of hope did he preach in the region of Decapolis, and how did those who heard respond to his testimony (Mark 5:20)?

_____

_____

The hardened and ungrateful hearts of those who loved their pigs and prosperity asked the Lord of glory to leave them alone, but Mark now introduces a well-known man and an anonymous woman who were thrilled to welcome Jesus to the seaside area of Capernaum. Their situations seemed as hopeless as the Gadarene's. Before we reach the end of chapter 5, this man and woman will be found singing songs of praise and gladness to the Mighty Conqueror of disease and death.

POWER OVER DISEASE AND DEATH

12. Read Mark 5:21–24. Who was Jairus and what urgent request did he bring to Jesus?

_____

What words of faith did he express in his desperate appeal (5:23)?

_____

_____

13. His heart touched by the need of the twelve-year-old girl, Jesus immediately left to help her. What delay did Jesus and Jairus experience in Mark 5:24–27?

_____

_____

This poor woman had been hopelessly sick with a blood disorder for twelve years. She had heard of Jesus' healing many others in her region and believed He could also help her.

14. What thoughts and actions did this woman use to express her faith in the healing power of Jesus (Mark 5:27–28)?

_____

After secretly reaching out to touch Him, what did the needy woman immediately experience (Mark 5:29)?

_____

She could keep no secrets from the omniscient One. What question did He ask of the crowd and His disciples (Mark 5:30)?

_____

15. After she revealed her identity, Jesus kindly addressed her, even calling her "daughter." Do you think the woman was now glad Jesus had not allowed her to remain anonymous? Explain.

_____

_____

She only touched the hem of His garment
As to His side she stole,

Amid the crowd that gathered around Him,

And straightway she was whole.

He turned with "Daughter, be of good comfort,

Thy faith hath made thee whole!"

And peace that passeth all understanding

With gladness filled her soul.

George F. Root

16. While Jesus was helping the one He called "daughter," what happened to Jairus' daughter (Mark 5:35)?

_____

The Master had comforting words for the broken-hearted father (verse 36). Write them below.

_____

This unexpected delay was puzzling and perhaps even frustrating to Jairus. Our own delays are also difficult to endure, are they not? Like Mary and Martha in John 11, we often exclaim, "Lord, if only you had not delayed, our brother would not have died." How might Jesus' words to Jairus encourage us when we're faced with unexpected delays to our requests?

17. Read Mark 5:40. What was the response of the unbelieving mourners to Jesus' words about the little girl's condition?

_____

Why did their mocking laughter not last very long (Mark 5:41–43)?

_____

Let us see in this miracle proof of what Jesus can do for dead souls. He can raise our children who are dead in sins, and make them walk before Him in newness of life. He can take our sons and daughters by the hand and say to them, "Get up," and tell them to live not for themselves but for Him who died for them and rose again. Have we a dead soul in our family? Let us call on the Lord to come and bring him to life (Ephesians 2:1, 5).[2]

THE SIN OF UNBELIEF

The Lord had, and still has, all power in heaven and earth (Matthew 28:18), but He never forced people to believe in Him and His message. Countless men and women chose to reject Him, and they still do. In this lesson we've already seen one example of rejection in Gadara. Another example is before us in Mark 6:1–6, and this one surely grieved Him greatly.

18. Read Mark 6:1–3. On what was to be His last visit to Nazareth, what ministry did Jesus have on the Sabbath?

What was the rude response He received from His family and hometown friends (Mark 6:2–3)?

These people knew all about Jesus and His background. They believed that knowing Jesus' past gave them a complete understanding of all His character and potential. They believed that one could only be whatever his father had been. The idea that a carpenter presumed to be a theologian upset them; that function was reserved for those officially appointed because of family connections and education.[3]

The Nazarenes refused to believe Jesus was anything but a hometown boy. In their minds, He certainly was not a teacher come from God.

19. What blessings did their sinful unbelief cost them (Mark 6:5)?

Not all in Nazareth were unbelievers, however. How was the faith of a few folks rewarded (Mark 6:5)?

20. Throngs of men and women in Galilee had marveled at Jesus' words and wonders. In Mark 6:6, what caused the Master to marvel at the Nazarenes?

What unbelief in our lives may also cause Him to marvel?
Explain.

_____

_____

THINK ON THESE THINGS

✢ Jesus' disciples were not exempt from storms, and neither are
we. When we are tossed up and down by dangerous winds and
waves, may we hold onto the promises our Master has given us.
"When the waves thereof arise, thou stillest them" (Psalm 89:9).
Can our little boat sink while the dear Lord is in it? "Be still
my soul! The waves and winds *still* know His voice Who ruled
them while He dwelt below!"

✢ Think of it! The once-demonic man of Gadara became an
evangelist! Only Jesus can free men from the chains of the
Wicked One, giving new life and a place to serve in His family.
What He did for the once-feared resident of the cemetery He
can do for each of us who knows Him as Savior.

Long ago the godly hymn writer Charles Wesley put into
words the testimony of the man of Gadara. Wesley's words also
describe what He did for us, don't they?

> *Long my imprisoned spirit lay,*
> *Fast bound in sin and nature's night.*
> *Thine eye diffused a quickening ray;*
> *I woke—the dungeon flamed with light!*
> *My chains fell off, my heart was free,*
> *I rose, went forth, and followed Thee!*

✢ God considers the sin of unbelief to be exceedingly sinful.
Wherever this heinous sin raises its head in the Old or New
Testaments, it is rebuked.

Let us watch our own hearts carefully in the matter of
unbelief. It is neither the lack of evidence nor the difficulties
of Christian doctrine that make people unbelievers. It is their
lack of will to believe. *They love sin. They are wedded to the
world.* In such a state of mind they never lack for reasons to
confirm their root of unbelief.[4]

✛ What work is God unable to do in our lives, our homes,
churches, and ministries because of unbelief? We must "take
heed, lest there be in any of [us] an evil heart of unbelief, in de-
parting from the living God" (Hebrews 3:12).

SHADOW SERVANTS

Those Who Served with Charles H. Spurgeon—
Anne Hillyard

After reading her copy of Charles Spurgeon's monthly publication, *The Sword and Trowel*, in August 1866, Mrs. Anne Hillyard
began praying about a project dear to her pastor's heart. During
Victorian times, there were countless orphaned children on the
streets of London. Spurgeon believed his huge church should be
doing more for these children. He asked his people to pray about
beginning a new work among the young and homeless, and he
asked them to plead with God that the money for building such a
work would be sent in. Mrs. Hillyard heard of the need and knew
she wanted to help.

In late August 1866, she contacted her pastor from her modest
Islington home, expressing the desire to contribute a very large and
generous amount of money toward the orphanage ministry. In a
follow-up letter to Spurgeon she wrote:

> God has graciously given me an unceasing longing to do His
> will in the matter [of the orphanage]. My oft-repeated prayer
> has been, "What shall I render unto the Lord for all of his
> benefits toward me" (Psalm 116:12)? I have now [a large gift]
> which I should like, God willing, to devote to the training
> and education of a few orphan boys. Bringing the little ones to

Jesus is my first and chief desire. I shall esteem it a great favor if you can visit and talk the matter over with me.[5]

The desired meeting was held, and Spurgeon and his assistant questioned Mrs. Hillyard carefully to be sure the money should not be given to relatives or even other ministries. The humble church member declared again that she wanted to entrust the entire amount to Spurgeon, and to him alone.

By January 1867 the land for the proposed orphanage was purchased in Stockwell, South London. The gift from Mrs. Hillyard was only the first of many small and large donations used to erect the needed buildings. Soon, seven dormitories, each housing thirty boys and a godly matron, were built and furnished. Donations were also received for the building of a headmaster's house, dining hall, gymnasium, and infirmary. In 1880 similar buildings were also funded for the care of homeless girls, and Mrs. Hillyard was again the first donor for the project.

The orphanage received fatherless boys and girls between the ages of six and ten. The children received daily spiritual instruction, a good English education, and job skills. The children were assigned work duties in their dormitory. No outside help was needed because the children did all the work. As they grew old enough, usually age fourteen, many employers desired to hire them as apprentices. A few of the boys eventually became students in the Pastor's College, another ministry of the tabernacle.

Mrs. Hillyard was often found on the grounds of Stockwell Orphanage. She served as a board member of the institution until her death, and a stained-glass window in the boardroom pictured the initial interview between Mrs. Hillyard, Pastor Spurgeon, and his assistant.

For many years God used the Stockwell Orphanage ministry for His glory. Long after faithful Anne Hillyard and her pastor were in heaven, boys and girls were still being taught the ways of the Lord. The buildings are but memories now. Stockwell Park High School presently occupies the orphanage site.

With the outbreak of World War II and the evacuation of children from London, Spurgeon's orphanage closed. The buildings were badly bombed and fell into disrepair. But the generous heart of shadow servant Anne Hillyard is still remembered in heaven. God made note of the treasure she chose to give to Him in 1866, and her reward will be great. Can He trust us also to lay up treasures in heaven? If God has entrusted money to us, will we not use it to bring souls into the kingdom?

Lesson 5

LIVING FOR JESUS

*"And they went out, and preached that men should
repent." (Mark 6:12)*

Scripture to read: Mark 6:7–56

Some of the details and events in this lesson may cause us to wonder. For example, we may wonder at the strict instructions Jesus gave the disciples on the eve of their first preaching tour. The cruel and untimely death of John the Baptist may also make us wonder why our Lord did not use His power to deliver John. After all, John had spent his entire life pointing others to the Lamb of God. Shouldn't he have been spared from death at the hands of a drunken king and a hateful, adulterous queen?

The disciples certainly wondered, as may we, how Jesus could be so long-suffering with the multitudes that demanded His attention every hour of the day. Why would He have compassion for people that desired only His works and not His words?

Most of us may also wonder how Jesus lovingly put up with twelve men who were so often stricken with spiritual amnesia! (Actually, don't we walk around in that sad state more often than we'd like to admit?) Living for Jesus amid the joys and disappointments of this life may also bring us face-to-face with doubts and unbelief.

Perhaps the answer to our wonderings is found in Isaiah 55:8: *"For my thoughts are not your thoughts, neither are your ways my ways, saith the Lord."* Our simple minds are not in the same league with that of God Almighty. There are many things we'll never understand about our lives or the lives of others. Some things we simply need to leave in the hands of our wise God, knowing He "is righteous in all his ways, and holy in all his works" (Psalm 145:17). Perhaps the Lord comforted the loving disciples of John the Baptist with this truth as they carried his headless body to its resting place.

The lesson before us contains great instructions to help us learn to live for Jesus as John the Baptist did. It will also show us how similar our faith is to that of Peter, James, John, and all the other men in Jesus' training school.

LIVING AND PREACHING

1. When Jesus ordained the twelve disciples in Mark 3:14, what were the two requirements each man was to fulfill?

_____

_____

These men had been listeners and observers up to this point. They had matured enough that Jesus now announced He would send them forth for their first attempt at preaching. We can call this exam time for a very privileged group of students.

2. Read Mark 6:7–11. Into what size ministry teams were the men to be divided?

_____

If you were choosing the teams, whom would you have put together? Why? You will find the names of all twelve in Mark 3:16–19.

_____

_____

_____

What were the men to take, or not take, with them? What do you think Jesus was trying to teach the men regarding their needs and accommodations for the trip?

_____

3. Jesus armed His disciples with might and miracles. But what message did He especially send them out to preach? See Mark 6:12.

_____

_____

4. With the mighty power of God upon them, what outstanding successes does Mark 6:13 say they experienced?

_____

A definition I have written in my Bible is that repentance is a turning away from sin, to God, that results in righteous living. Right in the middle of the disciples' big preaching tour, the Holy Spirit placed the sad and sobering story of sinners who would not repent! The primary message of John the Baptist had been repentance and belief on "the Lamb of God, which taketh away the sin of the world" (John 1:29). John had preached this unpopular message to thousands, including Herod.

LIVING AND DYING

5. Read Mark 6:14–16. When the news of Jesus' ministry reached Herod's palace, who did he think Jesus was?

_____

6. In Mark 6:17–20, the cowardly king was terrified with guilt of his past deeds. Why was Herod the king so afraid of his prisoner?

_____

How did the king's birthday feast turn into a scene of murder (Mark 6:21–29)?

7 Herod feared John, but he feared Herodias even more. In a few months Jesus would stand before this king in Jerusalem. According to Luke 23:8, what reception did Herod give the Lord?

What was Jesus' response to the murderer of His cousin, John the Baptist (Luke 23:9)?

Herod's conscience was now so deadened by his hardened heart that he committed what unholy actions against the Son of God (Luke 23:11)?

LIVING AND REPORTING

8. Mark dropped the story of Herod to continue the report of the disciples' preaching tour. Read Mark 6:30. What details did their reports contain?

9. Mark 6:31 records more of the busyness of Jesus and His men. As He sensed their weariness, what did He suggest?

A quiet vacation in the desert was certainly a welcome idea. However, it turned out to be a very short vacation. What was the reason for its brevity, according to Mark 6:32–33?

LIVING AND LEARNING

One of the Lord's most awesome miracles occurred in a desolate place. The feeding of a mass of people is the only one of Jesus' miracles recorded by all four writers of the Gospels. The same disciples who had experienced great victories on their preaching tour were about to learn they were not as ready for the ministry of serving as they had imagined.

10. We are reminded again, in the words of Mark 6:34, of the love and compassion the Savior has for sinners. As He saw the massive crowd, what opportunities did He see?

When the disciples observed the same crowd, what did they see (Mark 6:35–36)?

11. Read Mark 6:37–44. After organizing the crowd and miraculously multiplying the slim provisions, what happy and nutritious meal did Jesus provide for the hungry crowd and the disciples?

What after-dinner cleanup duties were required of the doubtful disciples? Why should the twelve baskets of leftovers have been a rebuke to their hearts?

Imagine five thousand men, plus women and children, sitting on the grass with all the food they cared to eat! What a scene for the disciples to see. How little they knew about the power of their mighty Master! How rebuked they should have been as they humbly collected the baskets of leftover bread and fish.

They were right to assume they had not done well on their first major exam after the preaching tour. But surely the feeding of the thousands caused their faith to grow. Or did it? They had little time to reflect on this subject, however. The night before them was to be an even greater trial of their faith.

12. After sending the crowds home and putting the disciples on a boat ride to Bethsaida, where did the Savior go (Mark 6:46)?

As we've seen earlier in Mark, Jesus' regular practice was to go to a private place to be with His Father. Do you have a similar habit? Why or why not?

_____

_____

13. Just as the weary disciples were on the boat and beginning to rest, what sudden interruption robbed them of their rest (Mark 6:48)?

_____

While the storm raged, Who did not take His eyes off them (6:48)?

_____

14. Mark states that the storm arose in the early evening. Why, then, do you think Jesus waited until between 3:00 and 6:00 a.m. (the fourth watch) to come to them (6:48)?

_____

_____

15. According to 6:48–50, in what miraculous way did Jesus appear to the disciples, and what was their response?

_____

_____

16. What comforting words did Jesus speak to the frightened men (Mark 6:50)?

_____

What is the meaning of the statement in 6:52 regarding their hearts? What does it indicate about the grade the disciples scored on their second big exam?

_____

_____

Should not the marvelous provision of the previous day have taught them to trust God for all their needs in future days?

Our panics of fear, and our transports of surprise, are both
evidences of weak faith. Let the great things which our Lord
has done for us have their due effect upon us, and teach us to
ask great things of God, and to expect great things from God.[1]

LIVING AND SERVING

17. Safely docked on the shore in Gennesaret, the men on the boat
did not go unnoticed. What busy activities did the arrival of the
Master initiate (Mark 6:55–56)?

_____

In each city and village where Jesus appeared, He was surrounded by every sort of disease and distress. What kind of faith
did Mark reveal about those who carried or led their sick ones to
the Savior?

_____

How did Jesus reward their faith (verse 56)?

_____

No doubt the disciples grew impatient with these continual hospital scenes. Perhaps they even attempted to hurry the Servant Savior
on to "more important things."

18. What truth had they forgotten concerning the reason Jesus had
come to earth? See Mark 10:45.

_____

As we will see in later lessons, many of the same people who
flocked to Jesus for healing wanted nothing to do with His message of salvation. Still He loved them and was their servant. Today
there are also multitudes who refuse His Word but are eager to
fly to Him for help when trouble enters their life. They will seek
earthly life for their broken bodies, but they will not come to Him
for eternal life.

THINK ON THESE THINGS

✠ The disciples were a privileged group. They saw Jesus' miracles firsthand and heard His words from His own mouth. But they could not remain learners forever, so the wise Master, in due course, sent them out to preach. After the preaching tour they entered their second stage of spiritual growth and development. The Savior also intends for us to learn and then to teach others. Have we reached this second stage of growth in our Christian life? So many believers remain learners all their lives, with no desire to teach or serve others. When will we begin to tell and share with others the great message that our Lord is the only way to heaven? Like the disciples, much has been given to us, and much is now required of us: "Unto whomsoever much is given, of him shall be much required" (Luke 12:48).

✠ Interruptions can be frustrating—especially when you are on vacation! I'm afraid my response to the clamoring multitude would have been similar to the one expressed by the weary disciples. We, too, forget that serving Jesus involves people and sacrifice. Jesus looks at people as needy sheep; we often see them as intrusions that deny us needed peace and quiet. The disciples needed an attitude change, and it is likely that we do also. Our hearts can become so calloused toward hungry souls, but His is always filled with long-suffering and compassion.

> *Soften my heart, Lord, soften my heart,*
> *From all indifference set me apart,*
> *To feel Your compassion, to weep with Your tears,*
> *Come soften my heart, O Lord, soften my heart.[2]*
> *(Graham Kendrick © 1988 Make Way Music. www.*
> *grahamkendrick.co.uk. International copyright secured.*
> *All rights reserved. Used by permission.)*

✠ Many believers are given to a collapse of their faith, especially when the night is dark and a violent storm is upon them. Eighteenth-century preacher and hymn writer John Newton lived and survived "many dangers, toils, and snares." One of his lesser-known hymns is one he titled "Begone Unbelief." I think his words are full of admonition for disciples of all ages.

Begone, unbelief, my Savior is near,
And for my relief will surely appear;
By prayer let me wrestle, and He will perform.
With Christ in the vessel, I smile at the storm.
Though dark be my way, since He is my Guide,
'Tis mine to obey, 'tis His to provide.
His love in times past forbids me to think
He'll leave me at last in trouble to sink.

SHADOW SERVANTS

Those Who Served with Charles H. Spurgeon— Susannah Spurgeon

On the morning of December 18, 1853, nineteen-year-old Charles Spurgeon preached for the first time in London. Susannah Thompson was not present as about eighty believers met to hear the young preacher's sermon from James 1:17. His message thrilled the small crowd, and most went out that afternoon inviting others to join them when the boy preacher spoke in the evening service.

To please her friends, Susannah was present as the enlarged congregation gathered that evening at the New Park Street church. She was not impressed with the boy-faced preacher, who kept wiping his brow with a large blue-dotted pocket handkerchief. She later confessed to being so spiritually dull that she failed to appreciate his great preaching.

Susannah had attended church all her life but was not saved until the age of twenty. She was not baptized nor a member of any church. She was very self-centered and indifferent to the things of God.

The deacons of the New Park Street church quickly agreed that young Charles should come to be their pastor on a three months' trial basis. Susannah began to faithfully attend services, and God used Charles's Bible preaching to change her heart. Within a year she surrendered fully to God, was baptized by Charles, and became a member of the growing church. He was her pastor for thirty-eight years.

As a member of a comfortable and godly London family, Susannah was well educated and had traveled in much of Europe. These advantages, along with her new godly life, prepared her well to serve God, not only as a church member but also as a pastor's wife. With thousands in attendance, she became Mrs. Charles H. Spurgeon on January 8, 1856.

The young couple plunged into a busy schedule of church activities. From the beginning, they were very frugal but very generous in giving to the Lord and His people. In less than two years twin boys joined their family. Charles and Thomas eventually became pastors themselves and gave their happy mother eight grandchildren.

In the early years of their marriage, Susannah had good health that enabled her to serve the Lord publicly. One of her duties was to send personal letters to all women candidates for baptism, informing them when to arrive, what items to bring, and what to wear. She stressed that no red flannel underwear was to be worn under their white baptismal gowns! Considering the hundreds of women who were baptized at the church, just writing all those letters, and searching out the dreaded red flannels, was quite a job!

At age thirty-three, Susannah had major surgery with a long recovery. She was close to death and never regained her full strength. Although an invalid for the rest of her life, she worked in the shadows for the Lord and the people of the great London church. Her special burden was the training of men for the pastorate, and she rejoiced with Charles when the Pastor's College opened. The first student, Thomas Medhurst, was personally tutored in their home and was helped financially by the Spurgeons. Later, hundreds of men studied and went out to serve on the mission field or in pastorates.

It was to these former students, as well as other needy pastors, that Susannah had a ministry. Mrs. Spurgeon's book fund began in 1875 when Susannah donated enough money to supply graduates of the college with a set of her husband's newly published commentary on the Psalms, *The Treasury of David*. What began in this small way continued for twenty years. When she retired from the book fund in 1895, she and her volunteer helpers had raised funds and sent out over two hundred thousand books and commentaries to poor pastors throughout the British Isles and the world. This great ministry was done in spite of Susannah's continual suffering and weakness.

Susannah joined her beloved husband in heaven on October 22, 1903. How grateful she was to have received strength to serve the Lord for the forty years she was a home-bound invalid. She was only one of the countless shadow servants who served in the shadow of the great Pastor Spurgeon. Serving together "under the shadow of the Almighty" (Psalm 91:1), this great army of servants brought Christ to countless souls in London and around the world. Although she was a weak vessel, she was strong for the Lord. On her tomb in Norwood Cemetery are found words from John Newton's hymn "Begone Unbelief":

> *Since all that I meet shall work for my good,*
> *The bitter is sweet, the medicine food.*
> *Though painful at present, 'twill cease before long,*
> *And then, oh how pleasant the conqueror's song.*

OPEN MY EYES

"Having eyes, see ye not? And having ears, hear ye not?
And do ye not remember?" (Mark 8:18)

Scripture to read: Mark 7:1–8:26

The lesson before us begins with spiritually blind Jewish leaders instructing our all-wise God in matters of religion. It will end with a physically blind man standing before our all-powerful Lord for healing. Between these two incidents of blindness we will read much about clean hands and unclean hearts; of hypocrites, deaf ears, a silent tongue, a great woman with a great burden, more mouths needing to be fed, seven big breadbaskets, ears that don't hear or understand, and eyes that don't see!

Before we finish, there will be important words about our own hearts, as well as our eyes, which are so often blind to spiritual truth. We'll also have instruction about ears that are very hard of hearing what the Master Teacher longs for us to understand. "Give me understanding, and I shall keep thy law; yea, I shall observe it with my whole heart" (Psalm 119:34).

"THEY FOUND FAULT"

We haven't heard from the scribes and Pharisees since Mark 3:6, when they plotted together to destroy Jesus. To help with that end, a group of reinforcements from the temple arrived in Galilee from Jerusalem. They were eager to see for themselves the "country preacher" they had heard so much about. They feared His popularity, and they came to find fault with the faultless Son of God. As Mark 7 opens, we find this unholy group spying on the Master and His friends.

1. Read Mark 7:1–2. What fault-finding accusation did the scribes make against some of the disciples?

    The charge was not that the disciples were eating with grimy hands but that they had not cleansed their hands with the proper rite of purification.[1]

2. What question did the religious leaders ask Jesus in Mark 7:5?

The scribes and Pharisees emphasized man-made tradition, that is, laws that were not part of God's laws. Over the centuries they had added so many man-made rules "that they were impossible to remember, much less keep. They specialized in trivia. In short, the 'tradition of the elders' (verse 5) was more important to them than God's revealed truth."[2]

3. Read Mark 7:6–9. Jesus had a ready answer to their charges. Of what things did He accuse them?

4. What did Jesus mean by calling these men hypocrites (verse 6)?

What does worshiping in vain (verse 7) mean?

_____

What had they done to the commandments of God (verse 8)?

_____

Religious ceremonies and rituals are not a sign of true belief in, and obedience to, God. True faith is not *doing*; it is *believing* on Him Who has already done all that is needed for our salvation. Praying, church attendance, and taking communion are commanded of believers. These are not done to earn our salvation but because we love the Lamb of God, Whose shed blood provided our salvation. It is always the Devil's tactic to substitute man's traditions as a means of salvation. This chart may help.

Man's Tradition	God's Truth
Outward forms such as:	Inward faith such as:
Bondage	Liberty
Trifling rules	Fundamental principles
Outward piety	True inward holiness
Neglect; replace Word of God	Exalts the Word of God[3]

"ARE YE WITHOUT UNDERSTANDING?"

5. According to Romans 3:10 all men are sinners. We are not sinners because of outward pollution but because of what? See Mark 7:21.

_____

According to Mark 7:21–23, what dreadful sins did Jesus say are found in the heart of every man?

_____

6. That which pollutes a man is his unclean, wicked heart, not his unwashed body. What truths do the following verses reveal about our hearts?

   • 1 Samuel 16:7

_____

- Proverbs 4:23

- Jeremiah 17:9

- Romans 10:9–10

> *O this faithless heart of mine!*
> *The way I know; I know my guide.*
> *Forgive me, O my Friend divine,*
> *That I so often turn aside.*
> *Alfred Vine*

"HE COULD NOT BE HID"

Jesus departed Galilee for a fifty-mile trip to the Mediterranean seaport towns of Tyre and Sidon. He blessed another home with His presence and desired to have a quiet time alone with His disciples. Mark reveals, however, that it was impossible to hide the Rose of Sharon, and soon a certain unnamed woman sought His presence.

7. According to Mark 7:24–30, how did the Gentile woman get His attention?

What heavy burden was on her heart, and what did she request of Jesus?

What was the meaning of Jesus' unexpected response?

Jesus' ministry was still mainly with His people, the Jews. The Jews considered the Gentiles to be no more worthy of receiving God's favor than would a common dog. The heart of the King of love, however, cares for all men. We have already seen Him show love and compassion to another Gentile in Gadara. Perhaps the news of the former maniac's deliverance had reached the costal areas. We do know that this woman was certain the Savior could deliver her loved one from the power of Satan.

8. Upon being called a derogatory name, most people would have left the scene. Instead, what did this woman do (Mark 7:28)?

_____

What did she mean by this statement?

_____

Some have questioned Jesus' seeming rudeness to the needy woman. Truthfully, these words do seem out of character for the Master. However, Mark shows us that His words were said with the purpose of testing her faith.

9. Read Matthew 15:28. Did this dear woman pass Jesus' faith test?

_____

According to this verse in Matthew, what commendation was given to her, and what words from His mouth especially rejoiced her heart?

_____

Mark 7:30 records the woman's return to her house. How had Jesus answered her request?

_____

"HE HATH DONE ALL THINGS WELL"

These words in Mark 7:37 are a testament to the greatness of the Lord. Some can do one thing well; others may be capable of doing several things well. But He alone does *all things* well *all* the time! On His way to Galilee, He once again visited Decapolis, a

Gentile area of ten cities on the eastern coast of the Sea of Galilee. Remember it was to this area that the new evangelist of Gadara was sent to tell of the great things Jesus had done for him (Mark 5:20).

10. Read Mark 7:32. Who was brought to Jesus, and what was his need?

_____

_____

What form of healing did his friends suggest Jesus should use?

_____

Jesus healed by *touching* a sick person (1:41), by *speaking* (2:5; 4:39), and by others *touching* His clothing (5:29; 6:56). But He is not limited to just a few methods of performing miracles. The method used in the story before us was very unusual—and successful.

11. Read Mark 7:33. Why do you think Jesus chose such a strange method of healing the deaf mute?

_____

What resulted from the Lord's unusual actions (Mark 7:35)?

_____

What a joy for the man's friends to hear him rejoice in his new ability to hear and speak! Surely he used his loosened tongue to praise the Great Physician. Surely he joined the astonished crowd as they marveled and declared, "He hath done all things well." Jesus knew, however, that in a short time, men like these would use their tongues to spit on and revile Him.

> *Hear Him, ye deaf; His praise, ye dumb,*
> *Your loosened tongues employ;*
> *Ye blind, behold your Savior comes,*
> *And leap ye lame for joy!*
> *Charles Wesley*

"I HAVE COMPASSION ON THE MULTITUDE"

We find yet another multitude of thousands gathered around Jesus in Mark 8:1–9. Please note that this is a similar, but totally different, event from the feeding of the five thousand.

12. Read Mark 8:1–9. What concern did Jesus express to the disciples about the faithful people who had heard His teaching?

_____

For three days their souls had been fed by the Bread of heaven. Their food supplies were now gone, however, and they were hungry.

What question did the disciples have for Jesus regarding this immediate need?

_____

A few days earlier, each of these disciples had personally collected baskets of leftovers after Jesus fed another multitude.

With that experience in mind, what should they have expressed to Jesus? What had they forgotten?

_____

13. Faced with sudden trials or suffering in your lives, have you ever forgotten God's past goodness and blessing to you? Explain.

_____

_____

_____

For good reasons, many commentators have said how much we are like the disciples. Looking at them is like looking into a mirror, isn't it? Like Peter, James, John, Matthew, and the others, we are quick to relapse into the sin of spiritual amnesia. O for a faith that will not shrink, even when it is faced with many trials!

> *Yesterday He helped me,*
> *Today I'll praise His Name,*

Because I know tomorrow,

He'll help me just the same.

Author Unknown

14. Read Mark 8:6–7. It is rightly said that our Lord is the Master of multiplication. As thousands watched, what miracle did He perform?

Before leaving for home, what activity did Mark 8:8 say the people observed?

We can learn from this activity that there is always a surplus when God is in the activity!

> The word *baskets* is a different word from that used in Mark 6:43. The two terms are always kept distinct in reference to the two miracles, evidence that different kinds of baskets were used. The baskets here evidently were larger than those used at the feeding of the five thousand. These baskets were like hampers, and [were] big enough to carry a man.[4]

"HOW IS IT THAT YE DO NOT UNDERSTAND?"

After leaving the quibbling Pharisees, who attempted to draw Him into meaningless dialogue, the Lord and His disciples boarded yet another ship. It is obvious that the disciples took none of the seven big baskets of bread for future meals. Perhaps all seven provided snacks for the contented multitude as they walked home. Jesus' plan for the disciples was another lesson about spiritual bread. Were their hearts ready to receive instruction?

15. What double words of warning did Jesus give His men in Mark 8:15?

> Leaven [yeast] in this passage symbolizes evil. As only a small amount of yeast is needed to make a batch of bread rise, so the hardheartedness of the religious and political leaders could

permeate and contaminate the entire society and make it rise up against Jesus.[5]

16. While He was thinking of the soul-corrupting danger of the Jewish leaders, the disciples were thinking of bread for their bodies. Read Mark 8:17–18. What stirring questions did Jesus ask His dull students?

_____

_____

17. In Mark 8:19–21, the patient teacher gave an exam. What were His questions?

_____

_____

What follow-up question did He ask in verse 21?

_____

Jesus knew Calvary was on the horizon. If His disciples didn't understand the meaning and the power behind the miracles, how would they understand His death and resurrection? He would double His teaching efforts in upcoming lessons. But, after dealing with blind disciples, He was ready to step off the ship to help a poor physically blind man in Bethsaida.

"HE PUT HIS HANDS UPON HIM"

18. Read Mark 8:22. Why was the needy man brought to the Savior?

_____

What method did the man's friends suggest Jesus use to heal him?

_____

How blessed was this man! First his friends took his hands and led Him to the Master. Shortly thereafter the Master Himself held his hands and also "put his hands upon him."

19. What procedure did Jesus choose to help the blind man (8:23)?

_____

How was this miracle different from all the other miracles we have studied?

_____

Do you think this miracle was too difficult for Jesus to handle in one step? Explain.

_____

20. How well could the man see after Jesus restored him (Mark 8:25)?

_____

THINK ON THESE THINGS

✝ Beware of having a religious lifestyle instead of a personal relationship with Christ. In many areas of our country religion is a lifestyle. People attend church and regularly give to support their church or denomination. But their lifestyle is the same as their nonreligious neighbors. They hear Scripture read, but they hear only with their head, just like the religious leaders did in this lesson. Theirs is not a life of following and obeying God. Instead, they are happy to follow blind leaders and remain blind sheep.

✝ The shameless persistence of the Syrophenician woman was wonderfully rewarded. She is forever an example of faith that honors God. Is someone you love presently under the power of the Wicked One? How fervently do you pray for him or her? Do you fully believe, as the unnamed woman did, that God is able to deliver your friend or loved one from the power of Satan? Do you believe that God "is a rewarder of them that diligently seek him" (Hebrews 11:6)?

✝ God is the constant witness of our heart condition, just as He was with the hearts of the religious leaders and the disciples. As He observes our hearts, what does He see? Are you glad He is the only one who sees the wretched sins dwelling there?

> My heart to Thee I bring,
> The heart I cannot read;
> A faithless, wandering thing,
> An evil heart indeed.
> I bring it, Savior, now to Thee,
> That fixed and faithful it may be.
>
> Frances Havergal

✠ We rejoice with those in the Gospels who once were blind, but after the touch of the Master were able to see. Psalm 146:8 reminds us that "the Lord openeth the eyes of the blind." He is still able to open our blind eyes to understand His Word. He is also able to open the eyes of lost men that they may see Him as the only way of salvation.

Open my eyes, illumine me, Spirit divine!

SHADOW SERVANTS

Those Who Served with Charles H. Spurgeon— John Lewis Keys

Pastor Charles Spurgeon was not only a mighty preacher, but his pen was also mighty. As a young pastor in London, he began publishing a weekly sermon, popularly known as The Penny Pulpit because of the cost. The first edition was printed in 1855. Grateful readers were able to buy their weekly editions at the booksellers every Thursday morning, and millions did until the last edition was printed in 1917—twenty-five years after Mr. Spurgeon entered heaven! (He had often preached ten messages a week, so there were plenty of new sermons to edit and print.) World War I ended this series, yet it is estimated that one hundred million copies were sold worldwide in the sixty-two-year history of The Penny Pulpit.[6]

By the time of his death in 1892, Spurgeon had written 135 books and edited another 28. Many of these became classics and are still prized by present-day preachers. But how could a busy pastor, often in ill health, have such a writing ministry? The answer is twofold: John Lewis Keys and J. W. Harrald. These two shadow servants served side by side with the Prince of Preachers for most of his ministry.

John Lewis Keys was his pastor's personal and literary secretary as well as a close friend of the Spurgeon family. From 1867–91 all Spurgeon's publications passed through his hands. He also read and edited the weekly proofs of the earlier mentioned Penny Pulpit. Additionally, the well-known monthly church publication, *The Sword and the Trowel*, was also his to edit. Keys was a writer himself and often contributed articles to the paper.

For many years he had the blessing of meeting daily with Spurgeon at his home. "There he worked with the Pastor in writing and research, as well as performing a number of duties, helping to relieve Spurgeon of untold tedious hours."[7] He was also entrusted with the duty of verifying quotations and seeing that punctuation and other details were in order.

Perhaps Keys's greatest work was his research and editing of Spurgeon's classic *Treasury of David*, a multivolume commentary on every verse in the book of Psalms. In commenting on Keys's valuable help, his pastor said, "This volume would have occupied far too much of my time had not my friend, Mr. John L. Keys, most diligently aided me. With his help I have ransacked books by the hundred!"[8] In all three volumes of this great work Spurgeon called attention to the value of Keys's help.

We know only a few details of Mr. Keys's personal life. During the time he worked with Spurgeon, he also served the Lord as an evangelist and a pastor in small chapels in the London suburbs of Wimbledon, Whitstable, and Streatham. He was married, and one of his sons became a pastor after attending Spurgeon's Pastor's College. Like so many others in Victorian times, he struggled with ill health most of his life. His struggle ended January 7, 1899, and he was reunited in heaven with his dear friend Spurgeon. It was surely a grand reunion when those two great servants met again!

"My industrious amanuensis [secretary]," "My valuable co-worker," "One of the inmates of my study on many days of the week!" These are just a few words of praise that came from the lips of Charles Spurgeon when he spoke of John Lewis Keys. The great pastor and author knew that without his "valuable co-worker" so much of his printed materials would not have been possible. What a loss that would have been to countless preachers and students who have regularly looked to "Charlie" for biblical inspiration! Thank you, John Lewis Keys for your walk with God and for serving so faithfully in the shadow of one of the greatest pastors God has ever given to His people.

MORE ABOUT JESUS
LET ME LEARN

Lesson 7

"And he began to teach them, that the Son of man must suffer many things." (Mark 8:31)

Scripture to read: Mark 8:27–9:50

With this lesson we complete half of Mark's wonderful story of Jesus. Every chapter is fully packed with amazing miracles that brought hope to countless lives. And who can forget the classroom sessions with the Great Teacher? Over and over He challenged His student disciples, and the multitudes, to open ears to hear and do the Word of the Lord.

The verses in this lesson include some of Jesus' clearest words about why He came to earth. While we won't comment on all sixty-one verses, we will find here great food for our souls and encouragement for our hearts. From the opening statement on the deity of the Lord to the closing warning about a real place called hell, this portion of Mark shows again how loving and patient the Savior is with sinful men.

The disciples had followed Jesus for over two years, and what patience He had shown them! Sadly, they had listened, but they had not learned. Thus, they were not ready for the new revelations the Master had for them. Mark records, for our learning, Peter's greatest, and worst, statements regarding the Lord. Along with James and John, he also saw well-known Old Testament heroes living again and speaking with the Master. But while these three disciples heard the voice of God on the mountain, the other nine heard lots of complaining voices down in the valley.

We tend to feel sorry and impatient with these men, don't we? However, before we shake our heads over their lack of faith and spiritual understanding, may we remember the statement from lesson 6: looking at them is like looking into a mirror and see-ing ourselves. Like them, we are prone to wander, prone to walk in unbelief, and prone to enjoy being served instead of being a servant.

LEARNING OF HIS CROSS

1. Read Mark 8:27–28. What important question did Jesus ask the disciples, and what were their answers?

    _____

    _____

    _____

    What additional question did He ask in 8:29? What answer did Peter give for the group?

    _____

    _____

2. The word *Christ* means "the anointed one"; the Messiah long expected. If Peter's answer was correct, why did Jesus speak the words of 8:30? Why should such a cause for rejoicing be kept silent?

    _____

    _____

    For them to go out and broadcast the fact that He was indeed the Messiah would simply raise false hopes among the people who were expecting an earthly Messiah who would fulfill their political hopes. Only when they understood the relationship between His suffering and His glory would they be qualified to adequately proclaim Him as the Messiah.[1]

3. Read Mark 8:31. What specific truths did Jesus begin to teach His students?

_____

_____

Why did Jesus emphasize that He must suffer and die? Read Hebrews 9:22 for your answer.

_____

_____

In Mark 8:32, what well-intentioned, but incorrect, response did Peter have to Jesus' announcement?

_____

What sharp rebuke did Jesus speak to Peter and all the disciples in Mark 8:33? What did He mean?

_____

_____

Peter's earlier answer to Jesus' question of His deity was one of the finest things the fisherman had spoken. Sadly, his words rebuking the Son of God were some of his worst. His words were meant to keep Christ from the cross, to encourage Him to take an easier way to His throne than the way of the cross. These were satanic words to prevent the Redeemer from doing His Father's will. Yes, Peter accepted the truth about Christ's deity, but he rejected anything having to do with the cross.

LEARNING OF OUR CROSS

Shortly after telling them of His cross, Jesus began to tell them of their own crosses.

> With their increased information as to His destiny, the question was again set before them whether they would follow

75

or forsake Him. If they did continue to be His followers, it must be as cross-bearers and self-deniers. He has not altered His terms for our generation. Do we accept them?[2]

4. Read Mark 8:34. What three requirements did Jesus have for all who would be His disciple?

_____

_____

_____

Remember Jesus was not speaking here of salvation, which is all of grace (Ephesians 2:8–9). He was saying that we must prove we are His followers by willingly accepting these conditions as our life goal.

5. The apostle Paul commanded similar requirements for believers in Romans 12:1–2. In these verses what ultimate submission is asked of all followers of Christ?

_____

Have you accepted these demands of discipleship in your life? Explain.

_____

_____

6. Explain the paradox, or contradictory statement, in Mark 8:35.

_____

_____

7. What important questions did Jesus ask in Mark 8:36–37?

_____

_____

8. Do you think these principles of discipleship are too demanding for present-day believers? Why or why not?

_____

_____

_____

These truths of Christian surrender and sacrifice are often preached and sung about in our churches. When we sing "I Surrender All," are we making a true statement to God, or does He know otherwise?

> *All to Jesus, I surrender, all to Him I freely give*
> *I will ever love and trust Him, in His presence daily live.*
> *Judson W. Van DeVenter*

LEARNING OF HIS SUPREMACY

9. Read Mark 9:1–4. In these verses, what great privilege was given to Peter, James, and John?

_____

Who was transfigured, or changed into another form, before them?

_____

What two great men from the Old Testament appeared in person with Jesus?

_____

10. Mark 9:4 says that these two "were talking with Jesus." Only Luke tells us the topic of their conversation. Read Luke 9:31 for that topic, and write it below.

_____

_____

After recent conversations with His disciples, how refreshing this visit with Moses and Elijah must have been for Jesus. Notice that Moses was not talking about his ministry, nor was Elijah. Their conversation about upcoming events in Jerusalem shows us that the residents of heaven were also awaiting Calvary.

11. We now come to another of poor Peter's disasters with words! In his excitement, fear, and sleepy condition (Luke 9:32), he didn't know what to say about such a grand scene. According to Mark 9:5, what proposal did he make?

_____

What do you think he meant?

_____

Could it be that Peter was thinking Jesus' cross and suffering could be avoided if they just stayed put in such holy company? Peter would have been happy to begin heaven immediately, thereby avoiding any more earthly sorrow and sin. Like us, Peter wanted the glory and a crown without suffering and shame.

12. Read Mark 9:7–8. What immediate events brought Peter back to reality?

_____

What did the disciples see?

_____

What command from heaven did they hear?

_____

Moses and Elijah were godly men, but One far greater than these stood on that mountain. The voice of the Father made very clear the supremacy of the Lord Jesus Christ. In Him alone is our salvation. He did not need the help of Moses and Elijah to save sinners. We are saved only by the blood of the crucified One!

13. On the way down the mountain, what further teaching did Jesus share with the three (9:9–13)?

_____

What question did they ask one another (9:10)?

_____

LEARNING OF FAITH AND POWER

14. Read Mark 9:14–18. What failure caused the nine disciples and the scribes to argue?

_____

Describe the daily despair of the demonic young man (9:18, 20–22)?

_____

15. What two questions did the long-suffering Lord ask the disciples and those around Him (9:19)?

_____

_____

What command did He give in 9:19?

_____

Satan desires to destroy our children and grandchildren as well. Read 9:19 again. What is the best thing we can do to help those we love?

_____

Sadly Jesus' disciples were part of the "faithless generation" referred to by Mark. This painful scene occurred because of their lack of faith. Jesus had given these men power to heal (Mark 6:13), but their power failure came because of their unbelief. They had new lessons to learn about walking by faith. Are you thankful He never tires of putting up with poor disciples like them . . . and us?

16. What second request was made by the heartbroken father in 9:22?

_____

According to 9:23, what requirement did he have to meet before help could be extended?

_____

What tearful request did the father make to Jesus in 9:24?

_____

This father was greatly distressed at his sin of unbelief. His prayer now was not only "help my child" but also "help my unbelief!" Unbelief always robs God of His glory, and it also robs us of the blessings He wants to bestow on us.

17. Read Mark 9:25–29 and then describe the healing of the pitiful son.

_____

In verse 28, the disciples had an important question for Jesus. What was the question, and what did the Master's answer in verse 29 mean?

_____

LEARNING OF HUMILITY AND SERVICE

The disciples failed in their efforts to heal because their hearts had begun to trust themselves instead of to trust God. This confidence in their flesh led them to neglect prayer and fasting. They also failed to exercise, by faith, the power the Lord had earlier bestowed on them. Thus they attempted to make their own miracle happen without help from God, thereby dishonoring Him and failing to serve the man and his son. So much of our own spiritual failure is also due to walking in the flesh instead of the Spirit.

18. Read Mark 9:30–31. What truth does Jesus attempt, once again, to teach His students?

_____

_____

For some reason, they failed again to understand the truth of Jesus' suffering, death, and resurrection (9:32). Instead, what other topic was on their minds (9:32–34)?

_____

What question did our all-knowing God ask them in 9:33?

_____

Jesus undertook to teach the Twelve the law of humility and that in His kingdom those who serve are the greatest examples of Christlikeness. It is easy to fret when we feel our proper place is not given to us. As with the disciples, such pettiness always looks so unimportant when we bring it into the presence of the greatest Servant of all. We must beware of pride, which leads us to believe that the work we do for Christ is more important than the work of others.

LEARNING OF ETERNAL PUNISHMENT

We end this lesson with our loving Savior's warning that hell is real, not an imagined place. Yes, the Lord believed in a place of eternal torment and punishment for all who will not believe on Him as the only way to heaven.

19. In Mark 9:43–48 Jesus gave three hypothetical examples of the seriousness of sin and its punishment. What are these?

_____

_____

After hearing all the loving and kind words of Jesus in Mark, we may be shocked by these strong words that warn all men of the need to do spiritual surgery on their bodies. Of course, He does not say we are to mutilate our bodies. But we are to cut sin out of our lives wherever it is found. Because our hearts are evil, our body members can become instruments that lead us into evil. The eye, the hand, and the foot need continual watching or they will lead us into sin.

20. What description of hell does Jesus give in Mark 9:48?

_____

21. According to Revelation 20:15, why are people "cast into the lake of fire"?

_____

Read John 3:16. How can all men escape spending eternity in hell?

_____

22. These somber words on eternal punishment were spoken as the Savior's last message to the people of Capernaum. Read Matthew 11:20–24. Why did He pronounce judgment on this and other cities where He had ministered?

_____

Matthew, under the direction of the Holy Spirit, wrote these chilling words about his own hometown. Peter, James, and John were also citizens of Capernaum, and Peter's family still lived there.

How it must have saddened them to realize where so many of
their acquaintances would spend eternity.

THINK ON THESE THINGS

✝ Peter's answer to the question "Whom do men say that I am?"
is still the only correct answer. John, another disciple who was
present to hear Peter's declaration, also wrote this statement of
His deity: "In the beginning was the Word, and the Word was
with God, and the Word was God" (John 1:1). The Lord is not
one of many prophets; He is greater than them all. He is not
one of several ways to heaven; He is the only way (John 14:6).

> *Veiled in flesh the Godhead see!*
> *Hail the incarnate Deity!*
> *Pleased as Man with men to dwell,*
> *Jesus, our Immanuel!*
> *Charles Wesley*

✝ "How many times in my contemporary world do I read, view,
and hear the lie that to 'find happiness' I must 'follow my
dreams'? That is not what Jesus said! He clearly said that I may
find the real life for which I was designed and redeemed only
when I deny my own dreams of self-indulgence and self-glori-
fication and follow Him. Only when I lose myself and my 'life'
in Who He is will I find my own real life."[3]

✝ "For whatsoever things were written aforetime were written
for our learning, that we through patience and comfort of the
scriptures might have hope" (Romans 15:4). The book of Mark
was written that we might learn of our Savior and His plan for
our lives. What are the lessons from this great book that have
helped and encouraged you the most?

> *More about Jesus let me learn,*
> *More of His holy will discern;*

Spirit of God my teacher be,
Showing the things of Christ to me.
Eliza E. Hewitt

SHADOW SERVANTS

Those Who Served with Charles H. Spurgeon—
Joseph W. Harrald

Rev. Joseph W. Harrald was born in 1849 in the East Anglia area
of England. At the age of twenty-one he became a student at the
Pastor's College. While a student he planted a church at Shoreham
and was pastor there until the late 1870s when Spurgeon noticed
his gifts in shorthand and other office abilities. Harrald resigned
his church and entered another ministry—that of private secretary
to the "Prince of Preachers." To this great pastor he was known as
"my armor bearer."

When his ministry with Spurgeon began, Harrald's main duty
was to help with the pastor's weekly mountain of correspondence.
He answered countless letters weekly, and he was careful to weed
out any abusive or profane letters that may have wounded his
friend. At the same time he placed on top of the mail stack those
notes that were sure to encourage his pastor. Letters containing
gifts for the many ministries overseen by Spurgeon always called
for a singing of the Doxology! Such letters were always carefully
placed on top of all other letters.

Travel arrangements were another responsibility of Mr. Harrald.
Spurgeon preached throughout England, Scotland, Ireland,
Holland, and other European countries. Handling countless train
and ship reservations without a telephone must have been chal-
lenging! Because Mrs. Spurgeon's health did not allow her to travel,
Harrald usually accompanied his pastor on these preaching trips.

For most of his ministry the great Spurgeon suffered greatly
with painful gout, which is now known to be a painful form of
arthritis.[4] Such a condition was aggravated by the smoggy, damp

atmosphere of London. For relief he sought out the sunny climate of southern France. In 1879 Harrald began to accompany the pastor on these trips. In France his secretarial duties continued as he took dictation, handled correspondence, ran errands, took Spurgeon on sunny carriage rides along the water and long walks in quiet gardens. He often read to the great author from inspirational books as well as from others on varied topics. Quiet sunny days in France renewed Pastor Spurgeon and enabled him to resume his heavy responsibilities in London.

In the fall of 1891 Harrald accompanied his pastor to France for what would be their last trip. By the providence of God, Mrs. Spurgeon was able to join them. It was Harrold's privilege to care for them both, and he was at the great preacher's bedside when he died January 31, 1892. It was this shadow servant Harrald who prayed with Susannah Spurgeon and wired the news of the pastor's death to his church family in London. He also accompanied the body back to England.

London had seen many royal funerals, but they had never seen one like that of the preacher who had faithfully served the King of Kings. To accommodate all who desired to attend, four funeral services were held in one day. Harrald helped plan the services. The 11:00 a.m. service was for church members only; at 3:00 p.m. only Baptist pastors and students attended. For the 7:00 p.m. service only Christian workers and members of other churches could attend, while the last service at 10:00 p.m. was open to the general public. At these last two services D. L. Moody's song leader, Ira Sankey, provided special music. Every seat in the great tabernacle was filled for all four services, and Harrald spoke at two of the services. He was also asked to pray at the graveside services in Norwood Cemetery, where thousands gathered for a last farewell to the beloved pastor.

With the death of Spurgeon, we might surmise that Harrald's duties were finished. Not so! For the next several years he became secretary to Mrs. Spurgeon, and his main duty was to help her research and write her husband's autobiography. Mr. Keys also assisted them with this task until his death in 1899. By the time

Harrald died in 1912, the task was completed and he had moved back to East Anglia to serve the Lord.

It has been almost 120 years since the death of Charles Spurgeon. No preacher in history has had so many people read his books as did Mr. Spurgeon. There are more books authored by him still in print today than any other English author. For that we are grateful, and for two shadow servants who helped make this possible we express gratitude to God. Mr. Harrald and Mr. Keys delighted to "abide under the shadow of the Almighty" (Psalm 91:1). They also delighted to serve the Almighty under the shadow of God's great warrior, Charles H. Spurgeon.

Lesson 8

JESUS LOVES ME, THIS I KNOW

"Then Jesus beholding him loved him."
(Mark 10:21)

Scripture to read: Mark 10:1–52

Having left the crowds of Capernaum, Jesus set His face steadfastly toward Jerusalem and all that awaited Him there. Before
His entrance into that city, however, the Pharisees continued to
follow Him like a pack of dogs. This lesson reveals yet another
instance where they attempted, and failed, to trap Him with their
silly questions.

In Mark 10 we find God's plan for marriage and His love for little
children. We are also introduced to a very rich and self-righteous
young man, as well as two ambitious brothers. Jesus also gave key
instructions to the disciples regarding the pathway to greatness,
and His love for a needy man named Bartimaeus is recorded for us.

In the plainest words He had used yet in Mark, Jesus again
spoke to His disciples of the things that would happen to Him in
Jerusalem. Did they fully comprehend the words *mock, scourge,
spit*, and *kill*? We know from their future actions that they missed
completely the good news of His resurrection! The key verse of

Mark's book is found in 10:45. Here we are reminded again that Jesus came not to be served but to serve others "and to give his life a ransom for many." This truth the disciples never truly understood until the wonderful book of Acts. There we read of mighty men, walking in the steps of Jesus while serving crowds of new believers. It is good for us to remember what great men the disciples *eventually became* for the glory of God. Such memories help us to think more kindly toward them because in Mark 10 they still seemed unlikely candidates for the job of servants.

HIS WORDS FOR UNLOVING HEARTS

In their attempts to expose Jesus as a false prophet, the Pharisees exposed their own unbelieving hearts. In this confrontation, the Savior also exposed their false teaching regarding divorce.

1. While Jesus was teaching, He was approached by the pious Pharisees, who already know it all. What question did they ask Jesus in Mark 10:2, and what was the main purpose of their inquiry?

    _____

    _____

2. Instead of falling into the trap they had set, what question did He ask them (10:3)?

    _____

    According to Jesus, why had Moses allowed for divorce approval to be given (10:4–5)?

    _____

3. Read Mark 10:6–9. The word *but* in verse 6 means a contrast between their view of marriage and God's view. What did Jesus tell them about marriage as God meant it to be?

    _____

    _____

God meant marriage to be permanent. Divorce is the breaking apart of something meant to be forever. What are some of the damages that occur when a home is broken apart?

_____

_____

Here our Lord appears as the defender of women and the lifter up of her head. Woman, according to our Lord's teaching, is not man's slave or toy, to be dismissed and cast off at the merest whim and caprice; she is man's complement and counterpart; and matrimony is a holy estate, in which woman has equal rights with man. The honor and respect paid to women today is owed chiefly, if not entirely, to the influence of Jesus.[1]

4. How does divorce affect our society? How does it affect our churches?

_____

_____

_____

What can we do to help and encourage those who suffer from a divorce?

_____

_____

God can forgive divorce as well as other sins. Divorce may sometimes be the lesser of two evils, but it is never pleasing to God or good in itself. It should not be looked upon by conscientious Christians as the preferred option.[2]

HIS LOVING HEART FOR CHILDREN

After another round with the hardhearted religious leaders, Jesus' next encounter must have cheered His heart. Usually people came to Him asking for deliverance or help with a physical malady. The little boys and girls, who were brought by their parents to see the gentle friend of all children, asked only to be in His presence.

5.   Read Mark 10:13–16. Why were young children brought to Jesus?

_____

When the disciples saw this scene, how did they respond?

_____

What was the response of Jesus to His men, and what command did He speak to them?

_____

_____

As the little children came closer, how did Jesus receive them?

_____

Did these children and their parents ever forget the time Jesus put His hands on them? O those mighty arms that so gently held them and the lovely hands that caressed them.

6.   Thus far in Mark we have seen the hands of Jesus touch many. Read the following verses and record below those who received His touch.

- Mark 1:31

_____

- Mark 1:41

_____

- Mark 5:41

_____

- Mark 7:33

_____

- Mark 9:27

_____

> _I think when I read that sweet story of old,_
> _When Jesus was here among men,_
> _How He called little children as lambs to His fold,_
> _I should like to have been with Him then._

I wish that His hands had been placed on my head,

That His arms had been thrown around me,

And that I might have seen His kind look

When He said, "Let the little ones come unto Me."

Jemima T. Luke

HIS LOVING HEART FOR UNBELIEVERS

7. Read Mark 10:17. Who was the young man who hurriedly ran to Jesus? What question did he have for the Master?

    _____

    Read his question again. What words stand out to you? Why?

    _____

    _____

8. What unexpected question did Jesus ask the young man in 10:18?

    _____

9. When confronted by the Lord with a list of commandments to keep, what was the young man's response (10:20)?

    _____

Here was an honest, but self-righteous, seeker of truth. Since coming of age he said with certainty that he had kept all the laws mentioned. Outwardly perhaps he had, but Jesus, Who could see his heart, knew otherwise. Thus Jesus began to prove to him that he had not kept the law at all.

10. Read Mark 10:21–22. After hearing his words, what did Jesus express toward this young man?

    _____

    What was the "one thing" the man lacked for eternal life?

    _____

    He had hoped his good works would give assurance of eternal life. According to 1 John 5:11, how do we know he was clinging to the wrong source?

    _____

He who had hurried to speak with the Master now walked away grieving. Why?

_____

_____

He longed for God's blessings but not for God. His time with Christ forced him to admit what he valued most. He rejected the One Whose "love passes knowledge" (Ephesians 3:19). He could have surrendered all, but he would not. Scripture is silent on his final destiny.

11. Jesus requires a surrendered heart and life from all who will follow Him. Are there any material possessions, career opportunities, or lifestyle choices that you are not willing to surrender to Christ? Explain.

_____

_____

12. In Mark 10:23–26 we find Jesus teaching His disciples "astonishing" things. What were these truths?

   • Verse 23

_____

   • Verse 24

_____

   • Verse 25

_____

13. Perhaps you know of people you feel will never be saved. Rich as well as poor sinners may seem unlikely to seek the Savior. Can you think of someone like that right now? While his or her salvation may seem impossible, what hope does Jesus give in 10:27?

_____

14. In Mark 10:29–30, what promise did God give to those who willingly surrender all to follow Him?

_____

What similar promise is found in Matthew 6:33 and Psalm 84:11?

HIS LOVING HEART FOR THE WORLD

As they struggled to understand His teaching about the rich, Jesus then reminded the disciples again of why they were going to Jerusalem. In His plainest words yet, He told them of the sorrows awaiting Him.

15. Read Mark 10:32–34. What events did the Savior say would occur upon their arrival in the city?

At least two other times (Mark 8:31; 9:31) they had heard similar words. According to Luke 18:34, what was their response to the sobering news?

Why do you think the news was so hard for them to comprehend?

HIS LOVING HEART FOR THE DISCIPLES

As Jesus continued steadfastly toward Jerusalem and death, His disciples followed along. However, they looked at Jerusalem as the place Jesus would be the Lion of Judah ruling His kingdom. Little did they understand that He would, instead, be the sacrificial Lamb, Whose blood would provide eternal life for all who believe in Him.

16. After hearing the Lord speak of upcoming events in Jerusalem, what untimely honor did brothers James and John seek for themselves (Mark 10:35–37)?

According to Matthew 20:20–21, who joined them in their desire for a greater place of honor?

17. What was Jesus' kind, but puzzling, answer to His ambitious disciples (Mark 10:38)?

When He spoke of a cup and a baptism, to what was He referring? Read Mark 14:36 for help with your answer.

What was the self-confident answer of James and John (Mark 10:39)?

18. In the last part of 10:39, Jesus prophesied about their future. What did He mean?

Read Acts 12:1–2 and Revelation 1:9. How was Jesus' prophesy fulfilled?

19. Read Mark 10:42–44. In verse 42 Jesus said the world thinks a person is great when he or she has others serving him or her. What was Jesus' formula of greatness for all who follow Him?

20. According to Mark 10:45 and Philippians 2:5–8, who is the supreme example of a servant?

21. Read the following words from Moses and tell what each verse says about serving God:

• Deuteronomy 6:13

• Deuteronomy 10:12

- Deuteronomy 10:20

- Deuteronomy 11:13

- Deuteronomy 13:4

HIS LOVING HEART FOR BARTIMAEUS

Earlier we met a rich man who became poor because he refused "the unsearchable riches of Christ" (Ephesians 3:8). Mark now introduces us to a poor man outside Jericho who came to know "the riches of his grace" (Ephesians 1:7).

22. Read Mark 10:46–52. What was Blind Bart's response to the news that Jesus was passing near him?

How did the crowd respond to his cries, and did this deter him?

What attention did his unceasing cries produce?

What conversation did Jesus and Bartimaeus share, and how did the Master help him?

After his life-changing miracle he was a man with new vision and a new calling. What did he begin to do?

Think of the things Bartimaeus's newly opened eyes would see if he followed his friend Jesus throughout the week ahead. Was he there when they crucified the Lord? Was he there when He rose from the grave? The story of Bartimaeus is the last recorded healing miracle in the book of Mark.

THINK ON THESE THINGS

✝ A good marriage takes three: a man, a woman, and God. If you have a happy marriage, what are you doing to keep it that way?

✝ If you are divorced, you should know that divorce is not the unpardonable sin, for there is mercy with the Lord. If a divorce is in your past, you need to be a part of a Bible-preaching church where you will be loved and have opportunities to serve God. Pastors and members of such churches must counsel, love, and encourage innocent parties who have suffered through a divorce.

✝ Pray fervently that your children and grandchildren will come to Jesus and grow to love Him with all their hearts. Pray especially that their hearts will always be tender, teachable, and obedient to the truths of God. Pray also that they will delight to be in His presence, as did the little ones in Mark 10.

✝ James, John, and all the other disciples desired to be number one in the kingdom of Christ. This is often still true among present-day believers, isn't it? As long as any of us thinks we're somebody, God can't use us. It is only when we humbly realize we're nothing that He can finally make something out of us.

> *Teach us to resemble Thee,*
> *In Thy sweet humility.*

✝ If your family, neighbors, and friends were asked to name five character traits about you, would one of them be that you have a servant's heart? The greatest epithet we can ever have is "She was a faithful servant of God."

✝ In Victorian England, a wealthy household had numerous servants. The lord and lady of a large estate would employ all, or most, of these servants to run their mansions:

- Cook

- Ladies' maids

- Butler

- Gardeners

- Kitchen maids

- Upstairs maids

- Valet(s)

- Nursery maid and nanny

- Scullery maid

- Parlor maids

- Footmen

- Stable grooms

- Laundry maid

- Housekeeper

- Boot boy(s)

- Governess

The family who had this array of servants were waited on hand and foot. Would any member of such a family willingly lay aside his or her wealthy position and finery to serve the servants? No! These earthly aristocrats loved to be served, never thinking of humbling themselves to serve others. It is no wonder Jesus said "how hard it is for them that trust in riches to enter into the kingdom of God" (Mark 10:24).

But didn't our Savior do for us what these earthly rich people would never do? He left His mansion in heaven, where the angels served and adored Him. He willingly took on a human, sinless body, living in poverty, suffering vile hatred, and dying for poor lost sinners at Calvary. His humble life forever teaches us that it is far better to be a servant than a sovereign!

SHADOW SERVANTS

Those Who Served with George Muller—
The staff of the Ashley Down Orphanage, Bristol, England

The "five immense three story buildings all alike and innocent of any embellishment, with strict utility written on every stone"[3] are quiet now. However, from 1849 until World War II, each building was buzzing as soon as the bells rang daily at 6:00 a.m. Busy boys and girls, from infants to age seventeen, were up dressing, or being dressed, in readiness for breakfast and an 8:30 morning service. When each of the large buildings were at their capacity, there were two thousand parentless children to be cared for each day. (And by the way, the buildings were always at capacity!)

I have always wondered what kind of staff it took to care for such an army of little people. I've also wondered who they were and how they came to be a part of one of the greatest faith ministries known to man. My husband and I have visited Bristol to see the "five immense" buildings, which still stand more than 160 years later as a testimony to the faithfulness of God.

We've also visited the Muller House in Bristol to see the small museum of George Muller's personal books and furniture. Also displayed are lots of pictures with hundreds of youthful happy faces, always accompanied by very Victorian nursemaids and dormitory supervisors. What we did not find at the Muller House, however, were any names of staff members. While Muller kept precise records of every penny given to the orphanage, he did not apparently keep written records of those who so willingly served in his very large shadow. He was so concerned that God alone receive the glory that he would not have used his own name had it not been necessary.

Every staff member, and child, came to Ashley Down as an answer to the prayers of George Muller. Every penny of money given to sustain the ministry came as an answer to prayer. From the beginning, Muller covenanted with God to run a faith ministry. He would ask no one for money except God. How God provided for every need is recorded in Muller's own handwriting in valuable journals now stored safely at the Muller House. Neither he nor his staff took a salary. All their needs were cared for through gifts to the ministry. In today's US currency, those gifts would have totaled millions of dollars.

While these godly men and women are now enjoying their rewards in heaven, I want to honor their memory through this very brief article. They were people who left all to follow Jesus and to care for little children so greatly loved by the Lord. I thank Him for those who loved Him so much they were willing to wash, comb, and cut hair; give baths; wash and keep up with countless little socks, nightshirts, jackets, dresses, shirts, pants, Sunday suits, shawls, straw bonnets, white pinafores, and three pairs of shoes per child!

These selfless servants also kept the dormitories, schoolrooms, bathhouses, play areas, infirmaries, and lawns noticeably clean and neat. They cooked wagonloads of porridge, meat, potatoes, soup, and rice. They sliced mountains of bread, washed dishes, and saw God provide milk for every meal. They planned birthday and Christmas parties; took children on "fresh air" outings; taught classrooms of wiggly boys and girls to read, write, count, and learn Bible stories and verses. They taught knitting and needlework to the girls and gardening to the boys. And when most poor children in England had little, if any, education, the children at Muller's orphanage were being educated in spiritual and secular life skills—all because of God's faithful provisions.

God bless the memory of these unnamed, godly shadow servants! I encourage you to read more about them in the numerous biographies available on the life of George Muller. May their faithful service for God open our eyes to a careful appraisal of our own reasons for serving our Lord. How willing are we to leave all to be a shadow servant for God?

Lesson 9
PRAISE MY SOUL, THE KING OF HEAVEN

"Hosanna; Blessed is he that cometh in the name of
the Lord. . . . Hosanna in the highest."
(Mark 11:9–10)

Scripture to read: Mark 11:1–12:44

We will cover two important chapters in this lesson. If you count the total number of verses, you may dread even beginning! Let me encourage you by saying we will not cover all seventy-seven verses. I hope you will be glad, however, for those verses we do consider. Contained within them are two unnamed servants—one at the beginning of chapter 11 the other at the close of chapter 12. In between the story of these servants we will encounter a donkey, doves, withered leaves, a vineyard, wounded servants, dead servants, flying coins, overturned tables, and another important reminder to "have faith in God" (Mark 11:22).

Because this entire lesson centers on Jerusalem and the temple, we will study plenty of pious religious men who plotted to expose Jesus as a false messiah. Instead, He ripped off their false faces, exposing their vile hearts. As He addressed the common people who heard Him gladly, He took time to warn of pompous leaders in love with "salutations in the marketplaces, and the chief seats in the synagogues, and the uppermost rooms at feasts" (Mark 12:38–39).

This lesson opens with another event that is recorded in all four Gospels: the triumphal entry of King Jesus into the city of Jerusalem. This King even arranged for His own transportation! As He rode through the city, the crowd carpeted the street with palm branches. What a privilege for us to now join this crowd and see our King of Glory riding toward Calvary.

> *Ride on, ride on, in majesty!*
> *In lowly pomp ride on to die!*
> *O Christ! Thy triumph now begin*
> *Over captive death and conquered sin.*
> Henry H. Milman

BEHOLD YOUR KING!

Numerous times in Mark we have read of Jesus withdrawing from crowds. He often spent time in the remote desert of Galilee, not seeking any public honor from His followers. However, His very public entrance into Jerusalem not only fulfilled prophecy but also introduced to the Passover crowds the Lamb, Who would soon be slain for the sins of the world.

1. According to Mark 11:1–2, what preparations for His entry were carried out by two disciples?

    _____

    What specific things did Jesus know about the colt (Mark 11:2)?

    _____

    _____

2. Read Mark 11:4–6. What words from the disciples allowed the colt to be taken?

    _____

Which Old Testament prophecy did the disciples, and the owner of the colt, have the privilege of seeing fulfilled? See Zechariah 9:9.

What an honor these colt owners had to minister to Jesus in the last week of His earthly life. Their story reminds us that our Lord is still able to raise up from nowhere the servants He needs to accomplish His purposes. Dr. A. B. Simpson expressed this when he wrote,

> God is preparing His heroes; and when opportunity comes, He can fit them into their place in a moment, and the world will wonder where they came from.[1]

3. Read Matthew 21:8–11. With what words of praise did the crowd receive the Son of David?

4. After His public entry into Jerusalem, where did Jesus go first (Mark 11:11)?

When He "looked around about upon all things," what do you think He saw that pleased or displeased Him? Read Mark 11:15–19 for help with your answer.

When He looks "round about on all things" in our churches, what might He see that pleases or displeases Him?

5. According to Mark 11:17, with what charge did our all-knowing God accuse the corrupt leaders?

When the scribes and chief priests learned of His actions and accusations, how did they respond (Mark 11:18)?

As a twelve-year-old boy (Luke 2:41–47), Jesus had visited the temple and astonished the church leaders with exact answers to their questions. Now He astonished the leaders again by shutting down their highly profitable money-making schemes. Their love of money and self, and lack of love for God, led them to have supreme hatred for the King of Glory.

THE KING DEMANDS FRUIT

In Mark 11:12–14, 20–21, Jesus used a familiar tree in Israel to teach the disciples, and us, an important Bible truth. The fig tree growing near Bethany had beautiful leaves, but there were no figs to be found on its branches.

6. As Jesus and the disciples walked to Jerusalem, what basic human need did He experience (Mark 11:12)?

    _____

    Why was He disappointed with the fig tree (Mark 11:13)?

    _____

    What prophecy did He make about the barren tree, and how was this prophecy fulfilled (Mark 11:14, 20)?

    _____

    _____

Symbolically Israel was in the same pitiful condition as the fig tree. While making loud and public professions of belief in God, the genuine fruit of belief, obedience, mercy, love, and truth were sadly missing in the lives of most Jews. They had a mouth religion but not a heart religion. Their daily lives produced nothing but dried and withered leaves.

7. There is great danger of spiritual barrenness in our own lives. Read John 15:1–8. What does Jesus demand of every believer? How is it possible for us to bear fruit for our Master (John 15:4–5; Galatians 5:16, 22–23)?

    _____

    _____

    When we lack spiritual fruit, what does Jesus often do to cause fruitfulness in our lives (John 15:2)?

    _____

8. In Psalm 1:3 how does the psalmist describe a believer who delights in the Lord?

_____

_____

In your service for God, how are you presently producing fruit?

_____

_____

Is there ever a time a believer ceases fruit bearing? According to Psalm 92:14, when are we to still be fruitful?

_____

THE KING'S PRAYER PROCLAMATION

When Peter called Jesus' attention to the withered fig tree, the answer Jesus gave him was somewhat puzzling. An early morning teaching session took place as the group walked toward Jerusalem. The subject was a familiar one to these who were quite challenged in the matter of faith. Some of us who are similarly challenged will also profit from the subject Jesus taught in this class.

9. Read Mark 11:22–26. To receive answered prayer, what conditions did Jesus say must be met?

_____   _____

_____

Jesus had just spoken of a barren fruit tree. John and Peter would later warn against barrenness (John 15; 2 Peter 1:8). Can a believer bear God-honoring fruit without prayer, faith, and forgiveness? Explain.

_____

_____

10. The matter of forgiveness is mentioned twice by Jesus. Forgiveness is a choice we make, and not always an easy choice. Is there someone you have chosen not to forgive? Will such a spirit

hinder your fellowship with God and your ministry for God?
Explain.

_____

_____

THE KING TELLS A STORY

Having exposed the hypocrisy of the religious leaders in 11:27–33,
Jesus then proceeded to tell them a revealing parable, or story,
about a grape vineyard. Read the parable in Mark 12:1–11 and answer the following questions.

11. Whom do you think the following characters in the story
    represent?

    • Owner of the vineyard

    _____

    • Husbandmen (hired farmers)

    _____

    • Servant

    _____

    • Other servants

    _____

    • Well-beloved son

    _____

12. Read Mark 12:12. How did the religious leaders respond to the
    parable? Why?

    _____

    _____

13. Knowing well that Jesus spoke of their heart wickedness, note
    they did not repent. What additional symbolism from Psalm
    118:22 is used in verse 10 to reveal their rejection of the Lord?

    _____

As you read the parable, did you notice the love and patience of the vineyard owner? Truly His love for sinners passes knowledge (Ephesians 3:19)!

14. Read Matthew 23:37–38. What expressions of the love for His people, the Jews, did Jesus reveal in these verses?

_____

What prophecy did He speak against those who would not love and obey Him?

_____

Judgment fell on Jerusalem and God's people in AD 70. At that time the city and its residents were brutally demolished by the Romans during Passover week. The prophecy Jesus spoke of in Mark 12:9 was fulfilled in the book of Acts. In the establishment of His church, He used leaders who were, for the most part, Gentiles.

THE KING AND HIS ENEMIES

The next fifteen verses in Mark 12 contain more of the same malicious attempts to trap or expose the Son of God. With combined hatred, one group after another confronted Him, always hoping they could show Him to be a traitor to the Jews or the Romans. How ignorant are men in their foolish dealings with the holy, all-wise God. How patient was the Lord in His dealings with these blasphemers. Just when we are ready to leave the hypocrites to themselves, we read of one scribe truly desirous of learning from the Master.

15. Read Mark 12:28. Why did the unnamed scribe ask Jesus a question?

_____

The scribes were teachers of the law. What question did he ask about the commandments?

_____

How did Jesus respond to this question (Mark 12:29–31)?

_____

16. Read the scribe's words in Mark 12:32–33. What did these words reveal about his knowledge of God and the Old Testament?

_____

The Lord saw this man's heart. What were the last words Jesus spoke to him in Mark 12:34? Here was a man who came very close to the gates of heaven. He was almost persuaded, but only God knows his final destiny.

THE KING AND THE COINS

As Jesus sat in the temple, countless people walked past Him, most with the purpose of depositing their offerings in one of the offering boxes lining the wall. After all the wrangling with temple officials who hated Him, His next encounter with a poor, godly widow surely cheered His heart.

17. Read Mark 12:41. What did Jesus observe about the people and their offerings?

_____

What offering did the poor widow give (Mark 12:42)?

_____

18. A widow living in poverty had many reasons not to give an offering. In what way did she give more than any of the others (Mark 12:44)?

19. Since this poor woman gave God all she had, how do you think she was able to provide for herself? Look up the following verses to find your answer.

   • Matthew 6:33

_____

   • Mark 10:29–30

_____

- Philippians 4:19

---

20. In our churches today Jesus still observes the offerings people put into His treasury. What might He see that pleases or displeases Him?

THINK ON THESE THINGS

✠ The entrance of Jesus into Jerusalem is one of a few events in Jesus' life recorded in all four of the Gospels. Earlier we commented on the only miracle recorded by the four writers: the feeding of the five thousand. In lesson 10 we will find that several events associated with the Lord's death are also carefully recorded by each of the Gospel writers. When there is repetition in Scripture, it is repeated for a purpose. What truths from Jesus' welcoming ride into Jerusalem might He want us to remember?

✠ The appearance of unnamed donkey owners willing to share what they had with Jesus should remind us that He can *still* raise up servants to provide the needs of individuals or ministries. He can also bring across the paths of our unsaved friends or loved ones just the right servants needed to touch their hearts for the Lord.

> *Say not my soul, "From whence can God relieve my care?"*
> *Remember that Omnipotence has servants everywhere.*
> *His method is sublime, His heart profoundly kind,*
> *God never is before His time, and never is behind.*[2]
> *Charles Haddon Spurgeon*

✠ Peter, who was present when Jesus denounced the fig tree for having no fruit, later wrote about fruitfulness in the Christian life. (Perhaps he was remembering this incident.) In 2 Peter 1:8 he warned believers about being barren and unfruitful in the knowledge of our Lord . He preceded this statement with a list of character traits that must be added to our lives to prevent spiritual barrenness. Such a state produces Christians who are shriveled up and worth little to the work of God. May we ask God to make us fruitful servants instead of ones who are dried up and worth little to the Master.

> *Nothing but leaves! The Spirit grieves*
> *Over years of wasted life;*
> *Over sins indulged while conscience slept,*
> *Over vows and promises unkept,*
> *Then reap, from years of strife—*
> *Nothing but leaves!*
> *Nothing but leaves!*
> *Lucy E. Akerman*

✛ Every Christian has favorite Bible characters. In this lesson we met another of my favorites: the poor widow who gave all to God. Her name is known only to God, and I'm sure she never dreamed that her act of love would be recorded in the Bible for centuries of believers to read. Aren't you glad that the Holy Spirit directed Mark to share her testimony of faith and sacrifice for us? Long before her act of generosity, however, this woman had made God the King of her life. She had asked Him to reign over her, and her sacrificial gift made her love for the King of Glory obvious. What sacrifices in your life make it obvious that He is your King?

> *Come and reign over us,*
> *Ancient of Days!*

SHADOW SERVANTS

Those Who Served with William Carey—
Joshua and Hannah Marshman and William Ward

When the name of William Carey is mentioned, most believers know he was an early missionary to India. As a matter of fact he was one of the first to leave his homeland in England for "the propagation of the gospel among the heathen."[3] Other servants who followed in his footsteps, and helped reach countless Indians for Christ, are not as well known to believers of our generation. This is the story of three of those servants.

In June 1793 Carey sailed to India with his reluctant wife, Dorothy, and their four young sons— the youngest being only a month old. Dorothy's sister, Catharine, also accompanied the family to help with the children. Only she would return to her homeland again; the rest would eventually be buried in Indian soil.

For the next forty years, William Carey served God faithfully. The self-educated shoe repairman was responsible for translating the entire Bible into Bengali, Oriya, Marathi, Hindi, Assamese, and Sanskrit. He also translated portions of the Bible into twenty-nine other languages. Future missionaries and new converts were greatly helped and blessed because of Carey's laborious translation work.

After six years in India, however, the Careys had many serious needs. They had suffered from tropical diseases, and their five-year-old son had died of malaria. Primitive living conditions, little money, a strange culture, no friends, and unbearable heat were daily trials of their faith. Dorothy never recovered from these trials and suffered from mental illness until her death in 1807. With such discouragements, Carey could have quit and returned to England, but he gave thanks when God-sent shadow servants Joshua and Hannah Marshman and William Ward arrived in 1799 to labor with him.

William Ward was a thirty-year-old printer who had dedicated himself to be a missionary after hearing Carey present the need for laborers—especially printers—at a London service. Carey's last words to Ward after that meeting were "I hope, by God's blessing, to have the Bible translated and ready for the press in four or five years. You must come and print it for us."[4] Ward proved invaluable in Carey's ministry. As Carey translated, Ward printed. Soon the Word of God was distributed and preached. Ward himself learned several native languages and became a fervent preacher throughout northern India. In later years when a disastrous fire destroyed the mission printing office, Ward and the missionary team worked sacrificially to rebuild that important part of the Indian mission.

Ward's sudden death from cholera in 1823 was another blow to the small missionary family. This faithful servant of God, who served with such passion, was one of the first to be buried in the mission burial ground in Serampore near Calcutta.

Also serving in the shadow of William Carey were Joshua and Hannah Marshman and their family. They began their ministry almost as soon as they stepped on Indian soil. They contributed an astonishing effort to the ministry, beginning with the needful care and training of Carey's four sons, who were ages four, seven, twelve, and fifteen. Due to Dorothy's illness, and Carey's continual missionary tasks, the boys were unmannered, undisciplined, and uneducated. The Marshmans and William Ward took the care of these boys as their first ministry and successfully shaped their lives for God.

In the Marshmans and Ward, Carey found deep joy. He was especially grateful for Hannah, whose devout faith and cheerful temperament soon led her to be known as the mother of the Serampore mission. To earn money for the running of the mission, she and Joshua opened boy's and girl's boarding schools. The Bible was the foundation of these schools and of the free schools the Marshmans also ran for the children of India's very poor.

William Carey is rightly called the "father of Modern Protestant Missions." But we must remember that he saw very little success until he was joined by shadow servants William Ward and the Marshman family. Together they became a powerful gospel team that brought Christ to countless souls in India, and together they are buried at the mission burial ground in Serampore. These servants expected great things from God and attempted great things for God. The reading of their life stories will greatly profit all servants.

Lesson 10
LOOK TO THE LAMB OF GOD

"Behold the Lamb of God, which taketh away the
sin of the world." (John 1:29)

Scripture to read: Mark 13:1–14:26

In this lesson we will spend a lot of time on the Mount of Olives.
We will look at the Savior patiently teaching and warning of
things to come. After His discourse, the group walked to Bethany
to have an unforgettable time at the home of Simon, a leper whose
body had been cleansed of the dreaded disease and whose heart
had also been cleansed from sin. He gratefully invited Jesus, the
disciples, Mary, Martha, and Lazarus to a supper at his house.
What a privilege for all to be with the Lord shortly before His
death. Surely none present at the meal would ever forget the reason that home in the village of Bethany became "Simon's Scented
House."

The day following, Jesus and His group of men gathered around
another table in Jerusalem to observe the Passover. In an upper
room, so graciously provided by an unnamed servant, the group
experienced a shocking announcement. They also observed the most
awesome act of humility known to man. Later that same evening, as

Jesus instituted the Lord's Supper, one of the group slipped out into the darkness to complete his shameful betrayal of Jesus.

A LOOK AT THE TEMPLE

1. Read Mark 13:1–4. As Jesus and the disciples left the temple, what comment did one of the men make about the impressive buildings?

   _____

   What was the Lord's unexpected response to their comments?

   _____

2. What four disciples met privately with Jesus on the Mount of Olives, and what questions did they have for the Master?

   _____

   _____

   _____

Because of the wickedness of the Jewish people and their unscrupulous leaders, the magnificent temple would lay in shambles by AD 70. God would permit the mighty Roman army to pull it and the city of Jerusalem down stone by stone. It is only by the long-suffering of our God that many present-day cathedrals and churches are not turned into heaps of rubble. The true glory of a church does not consist in its buildings but in the faith and godliness of the members who worship there.

A LOOK AT FUTURE THINGS

Early in Jesus' ministry He gave what we know as the Sermon on the Mount. Here in Mark 13, He presented the sermon on the Mount of Olives to four of His disciples. Portions of the chapter deal with the destruction of Jerusalem and the temple; other portions speak of the second coming of Christ and the end of the world. Instead of dealing with the mountain of details and speculation as to when this will all take place, I aim to make devotional applications that will help ready us for the coming of our Lord.

3. Read Mark 13:5–6. With what warning did Jesus begin His discourse?

4. What similar warnings did Jesus give in the following verses of Mark 13?

- Verse 9

- Verse 22

- Verse 23

- Verse 33

- Verses 35–37

5. What do you think it means to "take heed" and "Watch"? Why do you think our Lord gave so many warnings to the disciples?

With these warnings "it is as if Christ said, 'Date fixing is not your concern. That is in God's own hands. Your business is to take heed to yourselves, to do your own duty faithfully and well.'"[1]

6. Peter and John were present when Christ spoke these warnings. Later they both wrote similar words in the books bearing their names. Of what did they remind us in these verses?

- 2 Peter 2:1–2

- 2 Peter 3:3–9

- 2 John 7

We later find Paul and Jude writing similar warnings. They, along with John and Peter, addressed the matter of diligent preparation for the Lord's coming.

7. In the following Scriptures, what did they say is necessary to be ready for His coming?

- 2 Timothy 4:5

- 2 Peter 3:10–18

- 1 John 2:28

- Jude 20–21

Bible scholars disagree in their interpretations of Mark 13:5–33. Some say verses 5–13 address the first 3½ years of the great tribulation and 14–31 address the second half.[2] Others believe 13:14–18 refers to the fall of Jerusalem, with verse 19 describing the final end times.[3] Whatever your interpretation, 13:7–13 describes the effects of sin produced in this fallen world because of wicked human hearts.

8. What are some of the effects of sin mentioned in Mark 13:7–13?

Mark warned in verse 7 that these events *do not necessarily* signal the end of the age but should be a warning for us to take heed that we live godly even when surrounded by wickedness.

9. Read Mark 13:13. Have you personally experienced hatred from others because you love and serve the Savior? Explain.

Read verse 13 again. Does this verse mean that endurance "unto the end" will earn a person salvation? Why or why not? Support your answer with Scripture.

_____

_____

_____

10. What comforting promise is given to believers in Mark 13:26? What are you presently doing to prepare for His imminent return?

_____

_____

11. What other encouraging promise do we find in Mark 13:31? According to Mark 13:32–33, what is the best-kept secret known to man?

_____

Men of every age have suggested they know the date and time of His coming. They have managed to deceive others into believing their theories. They have ended up laughingstocks, which is what they deserved. Study the Word so that you are not deceived by false prophets. Take heed, watch, and pray!

A LOOK AT HATRED AND LOVING DEVOTION

12. Mark 14:1–2 informs us of sinister plans the religious leaders had regarding Jesus. What were their plans?

_____

Why were these cowards hesitant to initiate their plans immediately?

_____

Here were so-called religious leaders plotting a murder! How they hated the One Who had exposed their vile hearts. We must remember that their descendants are still around today with equal hatred for the holy Son of God and those who love Him.

In the first century, the Jewish preparations for burial were quite involved. For the Lord, there would be no such opportunities to prepare His body for the tomb. We should be glad for a dear woman who anointed His head and feet with precious ointment ahead of time.

13. According to Mark 14:3, where were Jesus, His friends, and disciples enjoying a meal?

   _____

   What sacrificial act interrupted their meal?

   _____

   _____

   Who was the woman and why was her gift a sacrifice (John 12:1–3)?

   _____

   _____

14. According to Mark 14:4–5, why did some (especially Judas) find serious fault with Mary's gift to Jesus?

   _____

   How did He defend Mary's act of worship and sacrifice (Mark 14:6)?

   _____

   What special memorial did Jesus establish for Mary, and what did He say was the purpose of her act of devotion (Mark 14:8–9)?

   _____

   _____

   How did Mary alone have discernment to know Jesus was soon to die (Luke 10:39)?

   _____

A LOOK AT THE BETRAYER

Mark's lovely story of Mary's devotion was placed in Scripture between the plot to murder Jesus and the betrayal of Judas. What contrasts we see here! Someone has correctly said that Judas was *by* His side for three years, but he was not *on* His side.

15. According to Mark 14:10–11, how did the wicked chief priests respond to Judas's offer to help them destroy the Master?

"Why did Jesus choose Judas?" said an inquirer to Dr. Joseph Parker, a well-known pastor in London. "I don't know," replied Dr. Parker, "but I have a bigger mystery still. I cannot make out why He chose someone like me! But it was "Unto me, who am less than the least of all saints [that] this grace was given."[4]

A LOOK AT THE LAST PASSOVER

For fifteen hundred years millions of lambs had been slain in remembrance of the events of Exodus 12. Now the true sacrificial Lamb, Jesus Christ, was to shed His blood for the sins of all mankind. All the previously slain lambs had pointed to the sacrifice of the Lamb of God. For this last Passover a large room was needed, and God raised up an unknown servant to make this prophetic meal possible.

16. To whom were the disciples sent for securing the needed room (Mark 14:12–13)?

What words were they to speak to the owner of the house (Mark 14:14)?

How is this scene similar to the one we looked at in Mark 11:2–6?

The Lord has unnamed servants everywhere who stand by to do His bidding. Wouldn't you have been thrilled to be the owner of the house where Jesus met with His disciples for the last time? Perhaps you do have a room where a weary servant of the Lord can find rest. Are you willing to use that room, your kitchen, your car, or whatever you have, to serve God and His people? "All that thou spendest, Jesus will repay."

A LOOK AT TRUE HUMILITY

We know from John 13 that sometime during the Passover meal, the feet of all twelve disciples were washed. However, those twenty-four dirty feet weren't washed by house servants. The sovereign Lord Who "took upon him the form of a servant" (Philippians 2:7) took a towel and began washing grimy feet.

17. Read John 13:2–17. Describe the scene in verses 4–5.

_____

_____

According to verse 6, who protested the humble actions of our Lord?

_____

Why do you think none of the disciples had volunteered to wash feet?

_____

What did the Lord want His men, *and us*, to learn from His actions (verses 14–17)?

_____

_____

Is there anyone whose feet you would not wash? Remember, Jesus washed the feet of a man who would soon walk out to betray Him. He also washed the feet of eleven other disciples who would forsake Him!

Teach us to resemble Thee, in Thy sweet Humility.

18. Read Mark 14:17–19. What startling announcement did Jesus make to the men?

_____

What were their response and their questions for the Lord?

These men, who often debated who was the greatest, now questioned who was the vilest! To their credit they believed none of their fellow disciples could be guilty of such a crime. They did, however, distrust themselves, and every man looked at his own heart knowing they were capable of such a heinous sin. I wonder what Judas was thinking during this time, especially after he heard Jesus' words to the betrayer in verse 21?

A LOOK AT THE LORD'S SUPPER

Between verses 21 and 22 Judas departed to carry out his betrayal of the Lord. For the remaining disciples, the evening had been like none other. The feet washing had certainly been a never-to-be-forgotten experience, as had the startling announcement of a traitor in their midst. But before they sang a hymn and left for Gethsemane, Jesus established something that would forever help the disciples, and us, remember Jesus' death until He returns.

19. In the midst of the Passover meal, Jesus took two things from the table to share with the men (Mark 14:22–23). What did He say the broken bread represented? What did the wine represent?

Paul was not present in the Upper Room for the first Lord's Supper. (Perhaps He was in another part of Jerusalem observing the Passover.) Like the other religious leaders, he hated the Lamb of God and all who followed Him. After his conversion, the Lord Himself instructed Paul regarding the Lord's Table.

20. Read 1 Corinthians 11:23–30. According to verses 24–26, why was the Lord's Supper to be observed?

Before believers came to the Lord's Table, what preparation did Paul say they were to make (verses 27–28)?

_____

What sober warning is given to any who come to the table with sin in their heart (verse 29)?

_____

When the Lord's Supper is served at your church, how do you prepare your heart to participate?

_____

> *Lord, at Thy table I behold*
> *The wonders of Thy grace;*
> *But most of all I wonder that I*
> *Should find a welcome place.*
> *Had I ten thousand hearts, dear Lord,*
> *I'd give them all to Thee;*
> *Had I ten thousands tongues, they all*
> *Should join the harmony.*
> *Samuel Stennett*

THINK ON THESE THINGS

✝ In Mark 13:32 Jesus stated plainly that no one but the Father knows the day or hour of His return. Why is it that through the ages some have insisted they do know this secret? I have seen folks follow prophecy speakers from one town or one church after another hoping to hear some new theory about the end times. They neglect attending and giving to their own Bible-preaching church. They also neglect opportunities to serve God's people.

There is nothing wrong with churches having prophecy conferences. We have them at my church and they are a great blessing. But we need to remember the numerous times Christ warned His disciples about being alert, watching and praying. Without a strong foundation of Bible truth it is possible to be deceived by false prophets. Perhaps the apostle John had the words of the Olivet Discourse on his mind when he wrote: "And now, little children, abide in him; that when he shall appear, we may have confidence, and not be ashamed before him at his coming" (1 John 2:28).

✝ "What a waste!" said Judas of Mary's loving gift to the Savior. "What a waste!" many have said, or thought, of gifted servants who have given their lives to serve Christ in small villages or desert towns in faraway places. From family, and well-intentioned friends, these hurtful words have come. May the Lord deliver us from such statements when our children, grandchildren, or friends break their alabaster box and lay all at Jesus' feet. A waste? Never! Why are there not more such scenes of sacrifice?

✝ For the unknown servant who owned the Jerusalem house with an upper room, I give thanks. His willingness to have the room used by the King of Kings, when he might have rented it for a princely sum, revealed his heart priorities. What does the use of our time, property, children, and money reveal about our hearts?

✝ Mark 14:26 mentioned that before Jesus left the Upper Room for Calvary, He and the disciples sang a hymn.

> If you knew that at ten o'clock tonight you would be led away to be mocked, and despised, and scourged, and that tomorrow's sun would see you falsely accused, hanging, a convicted criminal to die upon a cross; do you think that you could sing after your last meal? Blessed Jesus, how fully were you consecrated to your task! Whereas other men sing when they are marching to their joys, Thou didst sing on the way to your death.[5]

SHADOW SERVANTS

Those Who Served with Hudson Taylor—Emily Blatchley

When the clipper ship *Lammermuir* sailed from the East India Docks, London, on May 26, 1866, it had onboard very valuable cargo. For the first time in Christian history, a large party of

Protestant missionaries sailed together for the shores of China. Among this group of eighteen adults were Mr. and Mrs. Hudson Taylor and their four children. As in the case of Mary of Bethany, some in England undoubtedly critiqued the entire effort as "a waste."

One of the single volunteers, Emily Blatchley, certainly didn't see their efforts to reach the lost as "a waste." After attending a women's training college in London, she also began a weekly trip into East London for prayer meetings for China. At these meetings she became friends with Hudson and Maria Taylor. It was to be a God-sent friendship lasting until her death in 1874.

The four-month trip to China was fraught with danger from two serious typhoons. Emily later wrote "in our hearts we thanked God for the great deliverance He had wrought for us in sparing the lives of all on board."[7] The *Lammermuir* limped into Shanghai in September, 1866, each missionary grateful to be standing on land once again!

The Taylor family unofficially adopted Emily as one of their own, and she became a governess for their children. She adopted full Chinese dress and lifestyle. Their meals were mostly rice, eaten with chopsticks. The Chinese shoes were almost as uncomfortable as their Victorian boots. The Chinese dress policy was unheard of until the Taylor's required it of their recruits. They were highly criticized back in England, but Emily wrote later that adapting to the new living standards "was all done with humility and as unto our Lord."

Emily taught the Taylor children their schoolwork, thereby freeing Maria Taylor to participate in more missionary work with her husband. She also became the "right hand secretary" of the China Inland Mission, taking care of mountains of correspondence between China and London. When the Taylors traveled by ship or carts into China, she traveled with them. God protected them against killer mobs who attacked, and would have killed them, in the Yangzhou riot of 1868.

In March 1870 Hudson Taylor asked Emily to make a great sacrifice and return to England with their older children. The Taylors felt these children needed, for health and education purposes, to live in England. Emily loved China and had given her life to serve God there until death. But she willingly accompanied the children back to London and served the Lord as their friend and governess.

The China Inland Mission was her life, so she became home secretary for CIM, which meant preparing, addressing, and mailing the mission paper. She was also hostess to prospective missionaries, served as mission bookkeeper, wrote letters to lonely workers in China, entertained strangers, and attended the weekly prayer meeting for CIM.

Emily struggled with tuberculosis during her last years in London, and her sudden death in the summer of 1874 was a blow to the young and struggling mission. At her funeral she was eulogized as one "unknown to the world, a true heroine with Christ-like self-sacrifice for others. Her life was consecrated to Christ and the salvation of the lost. None could have given more to the work of God than she did, for she gave all she had—herself."[8]

Her worn-out body was laid to rest in London's Highgate Cemetery, grave 20165. Thousands of London's well-known Victorian citizens are buried around her. Many have the finest marble statutes and elaborate granite gravestones. But the Lord's shadow servant Emily Blatchley was buried with a less expensive limestone marker that at one time announced only her name and the statistics of her life. After more than 130 years of London weather beating on it, the stone is now smooth, except for a simple carved cross.

On a visit to Highgate, a cemetery guide accompanied my husband and me to the grave, and we shared with her a little of Emily's life story. The guide was not especially impressed. But we were glad to place a bouquet of flowers on the simple grave. Such a small honor it was for one who was a mighty servant for the Most High God.

Lesson 11

O SACRED HEAD NOW WOUNDED

"And they smote him on the head with a reed, and did spit upon him." (Mark 15:19)

Scripture to read: Mark 14:27–15:20

A great Welsh preacher once wrote there were no Scriptures in all the Bible that he shrank from handling than those relating to the suffering and death of our Savior. "Sometimes I feel that the best and only way of reading them is to do so in silence upon our knees."[1] Somehow it does seem sacrilegious to break up the solemnity found here with questions and comments, but it is good for us to look at this great sight once again. We have heard these stories so often that they have become commonplace. May the lesson before us be a holy reminder of all that our redemption cost the Lord of glory.

Love so amazing, so divine,
Demands my soul, my life, my all!

PROPHECY AND PROMISES

After singing a hymn to close the Lord's Supper, Jesus quoted to the disciples important words from the prophet Zechariah regarding a Shepherd and scattered sheep. He also made yet another statement about His upcoming resurrection and a homecoming in Galilee. Sadly, His words went right over the top of their heads, as it had done several times before.

1. According to Mark 14:27, what would the disciples do that very night?

_____

What comforting promise was then given by the Lord in Mark 14:28?

_____

2. Read Mark 14:29–31. Why do you think Jesus singled out Peter for special notice since all the disciples said they would never deny Him?

_____

There is far more wickedness in all our self-confident hearts than we want to admit. As with the disciples, Jesus knows us far better than we do. All twelve of the Lord's men remind us there is no sin into which even the greatest saint may not fall if she does not stay close to the Shepherd. Solomon warned us in Proverbs 28:26: "He that trusteth in his own heart is a fool."

PRAYER AND PRIVILEGE

3. After Jesus left eight disciples near one of Gethsemane's main pathways, whom did He take into the garden with Him (Mark 14:32–33)?

_____

This privileged trio had witnessed the greatness of our Lord several times. What grief did they now witness in the garden (Mark 14:34–36)?

_____

According to Mark 14:34, how were they to occupy themselves while the Man of Sorrows spoke with His Father?

_____

4. Read Mark 14:35–36. As the Lord struggled in prayer, what burdens did He bring before His Father?

_____

5. In the midst of pouring out His sorrow in prayer, Jesus checked on His disciples three times. What activity did He observe them doing, and what important commands did He give them (Mark 14:37–38, 40–41)?

_____

_____

Realizing we are cut from the same cloth as Peter, James, and John, what applications can we make from Jesus' warnings for our own lives?

_____

_____

What did Jesus mean when He commanded them, and us, to "watch and pray lest ye enter into temptation" (Mark 14:38)?

_____

PROPHECY FULFILLED

It is painful to read of Jesus' betrayal and arrest by a friend, a friend whom Jesus chose and loved. From this poignant scene in Gethsemane we note Jesus going forward to meet His enemies. He did not hide from them. We need to remember it was not Judas who found Jesus that night; it was Jesus Who went out to meet him and his brutal bunch of thugs.

6. Read Mark 14:43–50. Whom did the cowardly religious leaders send to arrest the Friend of sinners?

_____

What hypocritical words and acts did Judas use to identify Jesus for the soldiers?

_____

_____

In Matthew 26:50 we are told the Lord's response to Judas' wicked actions. What was it?

7. John tells us (18:10) it was Peter who impulsively drew a sword to defend Jesus. What damage did he do to the personal slave of Caiaphas (Mark14:47)?

Read Luke 22:51. What gracious act of mercy did Jesus perform on the servant? (This was our Lord's last miracle, healing His enemy!)

8. Read Mark 14:50. As the great armed multitude led Jesus away, what prophecy about the disciples was fulfilled?

Mark 14:51–52 are puzzling verses, and this "certain young man" is not mentioned by the other three Gospel writers. Some believe it was Mark himself, but we will leave this to theologians to debate. The great English preacher J. C. Ryle said this in his commentary on Mark:

> It does not interest us much to know who this young man was, and it would not bring any very great fruit to us if we did know. If it had been useful for us to know, the Spirit of God would not have been silent, seeing that He is often marvelously diligent in relating very minute things.[2]

PIOUS PRIESTS

The work of the Wicked One is often done in darkness. The first trial of Jesus before the pious Sanhedrin is an example. After His arrest, Jesus faced a kangaroo court and serious witness tampering. There was nothing impartial about this phony trial. With Jesus in their hands, His enemies were smelling victory over the One they despised and rejected.

9. Read Mark 14:53–65. Briefly describe the trial of our great Creator at the hands of those He had created.

_____

_____

_____

Whom did they call as witnesses, and how credible were they (Mark 14:55–59)?

_____

How did Jesus answer their false charges (Mark 14:60–61)?

_____

What was their primary charge against Jesus (Mark 14:61–63) and what verdict was handed down (Mark 14:64)?

_____

_____

As He willingly yielded Himself into their hands, what unrestrained hatred and cruelty were leashed upon Him (Mark 14:65)?

_____

10. How are the events described by Mark a fulfillment of Isaiah's words in 53:3–5?

_____

_____

11. In Mark 10:45, what did Jesus say was His prime reason for coming to this cruel world?

_____

In the garden, and at His first trial, Jesus denied Himself any help from heaven. He had come to die for sinners and would finish that work at Calvary.

What help could He have summoned according to Matthew 26:53–54?

_____

_____

Here is love, vast as the ocean,
loving kindness as the flood,

When the Prince of Life, our Ransom,
shed for us His precious blood.
Who His love will not remember?
Who can cease to sing His praise?
He can never be forgotten
throughout heaven's eternal days.
William Rees

PETER

Prone to wander, Lord, I feel it,
Prone to leave the God I love.

12. Read Mark 14:66–69. Two servants confronted Peter as he warmed his hands on the grounds of Caiaphas's palace. What did each ask him, and what were his emphatic responses?

_____

_____

After being confronted by still others in the group (Mark 14:70), why do you think Peter resorted to cursing and swearing (Mark 14:71)?

_____

What a testimony Peter might have given! "Oh yes, I was with Him for three glorious years. He healed my mother-in-law. He saved me from drowning. With these eyes I saw Him heal and feed multitudes. Never did my ears hear Him speak harshly— except to those who did evil to His people. I was with Him during some of His most amazing events. Oh yes, I know Him and am proud that He loved me and chose me to be one of His disciples."

13. When the sounds of Peter's vile words melted into the night air, what reminded him of his Master's prophecy (Mark 14:72)?

_____

How great was Peter's collapse of faith! As he ran into the dark night, Mark 14:72 says that he did two things. What were they?

_____

_____

14. Thirty-three years after this incident Peter wrote a letter of instructions and warnings to believers. We know this letter as 2 Peter. Read Peter's closing words in 3:17–18. What important words did he write to help keep us from falling?

_____

_____

PONTIUS PILATE

Ecstatic over condemning their enemy Jesus to death, the corrupt religious leaders quickly turned Him over to Gentiles in the Roman government who were equally corrupt. The Jews could pronounce Him guilty, but they could not put Him to death. After a second trial, Pilate would order capital punishment for the spotless Lamb of God.

15. Read Mark 15:1–6 and briefly describe the courtroom scene.

_____

_____

As Jesus stood before him, what astonished Pilate? How did he know Jesus was no ordinary prisoner (Mark 15:5)?

_____

_____

Jesus' silence was the silence of absolute self-control. He simply stood there, like a mighty rock in a stormy sea, while the priests, like angry billows, came on and on, hurling their foaming accusations against Him, only to be thrown back by His massive, impenetrable silence.[3]

16. His choice not to speak was prophesied more than seven hundred years earlier. In Isaiah 53:7, what words did the prophet write concerning this very scene?

_____

_____

17. Like a politician, Pilate sought to gain favor with the people by releasing a prisoner of their choice during the feast days. Whom did Pilate want to release (Mark 15:9–10)? Why?

_____

_____

How did the chief priests interfere with Pilate's plan (Mark 15:11–13)?

_____

Although he believed Jesus to be innocent (Mark 15:14), Pilate was unwilling to argue with the cries of the mob. What did he do with Jesus (Mark 15:15)?

_____

PERSECUTION AND PROPHECY

O sacred head now wounded,
With grief and shame weighed down,
Now scornfully surrounded
With thorns Thine only crown.
Bernard of Clairvaux

When the jeering mob dispersed, the religious leaders returned to their pious duties. Only Jesus and Pilate remained. This man who knew the Lord was innocent still ordered a cruel Roman scourging for the King of Glory. After all that, the suffering of the Savior was not yet complete. He was turned over to a mob of Roman soldiers for another round of cruel mocking.

18. Whom did the soldiers who had scourged Jesus call together to help "honor" the "King of the Jews" (Mark 15:16)?

_____

A group of more than two hundred Gentile soldiers engaged in a mock coronation for the so-called "King." After reading Mark 15:17–20, describe what these wicked men did to Jesus.

_____

_____

_____

> *Did e'er such love and sorrow meet,*
> *Or thorns compose so rich a crown?*

19. Read Revelation 1:7. When King Jesus returns to earth, every eye will see Him. John said that one particular group will see the King in His glory. Who are they?

_____

The mocking tongues of the soldiers were silenced, but according to Paul in Philippians 2:10–11, all mankind, including these wicked soldiers, will one day pay homage to our Lord.

20. Isaiah 52:14 is a prophecy regarding the suffering of the Lord. According to this verse, how badly beaten was He?

_____

What a joke all this was to these callous men. Each one taking his turn smiting, beating, and spitting on the Lamb of God. Jesus is indeed the "man of sorrows, and acquainted with grief: and we hid as it were our faces from him" (Isaiah 53:3). We cannot bear the sight, and can we remain unmoved, when we know it was all for us?

> *What language shall I borrow, to thank Thee dearest friend,*
> *For this Thy dying sorrow, Thy pity without end?*
> *O make me Thine forever, and should I fainting be,*
> *Lord, let me never, never, outlive my love to Thee.*
> *Bernard of Clairvaux*

THINK ON THESE THINGS

✝ Earlier I noted similarities between us and the disciples. It is easy to criticize them, but we must remember that the Lord chose each one, fully aware of what he was. It is also good for us to remember what great men most of them became. Acts records their mighty works for the Lord. With what power Peter, John, and the others led and served the early church! People saw them and marveled, and "took knowledge of them, that they had been with Jesus" (Acts 4:13). Oh, that folks could say the same of us.

✝ Mark 15:16–32 is one of those passages that shows us

the infinite love of Christ toward sinners. The sufferings described in it would fill our minds with mingled horror and compassion if they had been inflicted on one who was only a man like ourselves. But when we reflect that the sufferer was the eternal Son of God, we are lost in wonder and amazement. And when we reflect further that these sufferings were voluntarily endured to deliver sinful men and women like ourselves from hell, we see something of Paul's meaning when he says, "the love of Christ which passeth knowledge" (Ephesians 3:18–19)![4]

✝ Each time we have the Lord's Supper at my church, I try to meditate on the prophet's words in Isaiah 53. Verse 2 of that great chapter always draws my attention: "He hath no form, nor comeliness; and when we shall see him there is no beauty that we should desire him." His bloody body did not faze the cruel religious leaders or the soldiers. They certainly saw no beauty when they looked on Him, but we who are called by His name should rejoice to say with Zechariah: "How great is his goodness, and how great is his beauty" (9:17)!

> *Beautiful Savior,*
> *King of Creation,*
> *Son of God and Son of Man.*
> *Truly I'll love Thee,*
> *Truly I'll serve Thee,*
> *Light of my soul,*
> *My Joy, my crown.*
> *Translated by Joseph A. Seiss*

SHADOW SERVANTS

Those Who Served with Hudson Taylor—
Mr. and Mrs. Lewis Nichol

In lesson 10 we met shadow servant Emily Blatchley, a member of the first group of missionaries to accompany Hudson Taylor to China in 1866. Later known as the historic *Lammermuir* Party, this group was the first team sent out under the authority of Hudson's new mission board, the China Inland Mission. Like the faith ministry of George Muller, it was another of the greatest faith ministries in Christian history.

As I write, I am looking at a picture of the *Lammermuir* Party. Surrounding Hudson and Maria Taylor, and four Taylor children, was a group of handsome, Victorian, young people. They had chosen to leave the comforts of their homeland for ministry in the interior of China. They had been warned about the primitive conditions and the difficult language to be mastered. The lovely European clothes worn for the picture would, upon arrival in China, be packed away in trunks. Hudson Taylor was the first to require his missionaries to fully adopt Chinese dress and living standards. Foreigners were not welcome in many inland cities of China, and thus native dress offered easier inroads into the hearts and minds of the people. "Full Chinese dress" was one of Taylor's hardest and fastest rules. It also would become a stumbling block for a few of the smiling faces who posed for the official team picture!

We know the names of each member of the *Lammermuir* Party from CIM records. On the front row in the photo are Lewis and Elizabeth Nichol from Scotland. Lewis was a blacksmith in his homeland.[5] The Nichols were undoubtedly excited to be on their way to China and had surrendered all to serve the Lord. It is with sadness I report that in two years, 1868, the Nichols, along with others they influenced, sailed back to England because of their own choices.

How did this happen? Dropouts in the ministry of the great Hudson Taylor? *Every* ministry, including that of our Lord, has dropouts. No one has stated the cause for this failure better than another CIM missionary who sailed for China sixty-two years after the sailing of the Nichols. Isobel Kuhn was that missionary, and here are her words:

> In October, 1928, when I sailed for China, there were eight or ten of us young women who sailed together. Those were memorable hours! Ruth Paxson, a veteran missionary sailing with us, agreed to an hour's Bible teaching every day. Standing in front of us, she looked into our faces and said, "Girls, when you get to China, all the scum of your nature will rise to the top." I was shocked. Scum? Was that not a strong word? All of us were nice girls, were we not? And so I was totally unprepared for the revolt of the flesh which was waiting for me on China's shores. The day was to come when on my knees in the Lord's presence I had to say: "Lord, scum is the only word to describe me"[6]

During the four-month trip to China, signs of scum arose among some of the *Lammermuir* Party. Sins were dealt with, confessions made, and harmony restored. In his early days in China, Lewis Nichol wrote

> The Chinese [dress] . . . has been a trial to me; but when I think it is for God and not man, it eases my mind; and that I also vowed to my God when at home, if He sent me to China, I was to count nothing dear to me but the glory of God and the salvation of souls.[7]

However, by the end of 1866, Mr. Nichol was the person responsible for causing severe disharmony among members of the team. He forgot his earlier vows to God and complained bitterly to anyone who would listen about Taylor's rules and leadership. His "scum" abounded as he caused dissension among his fellow team members and personnel associated with other missions. He soon refused to wear Chinese dress, and this offended the very people he wanted to reach for Christ. The local Chinese would not come to services because they did not recognize Mr. Nichol in British clothes!

As a few other team members also had "scum" eruptions, there was much heartache and the ministry was greatly hindered. Nichol's "scum" also found its way back across the ocean through complaining letters he wrote home. Hudson Taylor was aware of the problems and took himself away from the ministry several times to confront Nichols and the others. Before the end of 1868, Mr. and Mrs. Nichol were dismissed from service with CIM. Three single women under their influence also resigned.

What opportunity these folks had to serve in China with Hudson Taylor and hundreds of other pioneer missionaries. But they chose, instead, to serve their flesh. They would not "pour contempt on all [their] pride," but chose to walk in their scummy flesh, which can never please God (Romans 8:8).

None of us sets out to be a Lewis Nichol, do we? May his sad ending be a warning to our own lives, lest we also cause great harm to the cause of Christ. Watch out for the "scum"!

> *All the vain things that charm me most,*
> *I sacrifice them to His blood.*

Lesson 12
HALLELUJAH!
WHAT A SAVIOUR

"And he saith unto them, Be not affrighted: ye seek Jesus of Nazareth, which was crucified: he is risen; he is not here: behold the place where they laid him."
(Mark 16:6)

Scripture to read: Mark 15:21–16:20

One of my favorite Easter hymns is *Christ Arose* by Victorian hymn writer Robert Lowry. Each verse in the hymn is to be sung slowly and mournfully, creating an atmosphere of a funeral. But when the chorus begins, there is a great mood change as Christ's victory over death is proclaimed.

I feel that this lesson is somewhat like Lowry's hymn. Mark 15 begins with a mournful march of the suffering Savior through the streets of Jerusalem. It continues up the hill to Golgotha as the Redeemer is hung on a cross while wicked scoffers mock and blaspheme a dying man. Truly it was the darkest day in history. The chapter ends with a hurried funeral carried out by two friends who were members of the hated Sanhedrin. The loving care of these secret servants, and the kindness of several women, are true bright spots in the midst of this dark chapter.

As we begin Mark 16, the announcement from a heavenly visitor signals a time of great joy and rejoicing. Talk about a mood change! As the women hurried to tell the unbelievable news that Christ had risen, excitement abounded. This is especially noticeable if you also read the story as recorded by Matthew, Luke, and John. The day Jesus arose was the most victorious day in history because if our Lord had not risen, as He promised, our faith would be vain, and we would yet be in our sins (1 Corinthians 15:17).

"AND THEY CRUCIFIED HIM"

The Roman crucifixion was one of the most shameful and painful deaths ever devised. It usually followed immediately after the sentence of death, with the convicted felon responsible to carry his own cross. The Savior left the trial carrying His own cross (John 19:17). But because of all He had suffered, He soon fell beneath its load. No one in the crowd volunteered to help with His burden. However, the hardened soldiers sensed His weak condition and stepped in to hurry up the march to Golgotha.

1. What stranger did the soldiers compel, or require, to carry the cross of Jesus (Mark 15:21)?

God arranged for this Jew from Cyrene in Northern Africa to cross paths with Jesus at that moment. He was in Jerusalem to celebrate the Passover. Did he ever forget the day he met the true Passover Lamb on the Calvary road? Most commentators believe that Simon became a Christian after that brief walk in Jesus' company.

2. Read Mark 15:22–23. Why do you think Jesus refused the usual pain-deadening drink with myrrh?

3. Someone has said that gambling is the most hardening of all vices. Do you think the activity of the callous soldiers at the cross of Jesus (Matthew 15:24) gave proof of this statement? Explain.

The dice would be almost stained with the blood of Christ, yet the gamblers played on beneath the shadow of His cross.[1]

4. Read Mark 15:26. All the Gospel writers record the words Pilate ordered nailed to the top of the cross. What title did he assign to our Lord, and how did his words reveal the true identity of Christ?

How are Mark 15:27 and Luke 23:39–43 a fulfillment of Isaiah 53:12?

"THEY THAT PASSED BY RAILED ON HIM"

5. After reading Mark 15:29–33, describe the attitudes and actions of the people who saw Christ suffering on the cross.

What sarcastic demands did they make of the Lord?

The almighty Savior could certainly have saved His life if He had chosen. Why didn't He, and why is this so important to us? Read Hebrews 9:12–14; 10:10–12 for help with your answer.

> *On the mount of crucifixion,*
> *fountains opened deep and wide;*
> *Through the floodgates of God's mercy*
> *flowed a vast and gracious tide.*
> *Grace and love, like mighty rivers,*
> *poured incessant from above,*
> *And heaven's peace and perfect justice*
> *kissed a guilty world with love.*
> *William Rees*

6. From high noon (6th hour) to 3:00 p.m. (9th hour), Jesus hung on the rugged cross for our sins. According to Mark 15:33, what miracle touched the life of every person in the land of Palestine?

_____

Why do you think God caused darkness at this particular time?

_____

_____

7. Read Psalm 22:1–18. David wrote this psalm hundreds of years prior to Calvary. What prophetic statements found here are fulfilled in Mark 15:22–34?

_____

_____

"TRULY THIS MAN WAS THE SON OF GOD"

At 3:00 p.m. Jesus' loud cry of finished redemption was heard by all who were near the cross. Across town a startling miracle occurred in the temple. This great event was certainly heard by all who were present for the afternoon service!

8. According to Mark 15:38, what miracle signaled the end of Judaism?

_____

[At 3:00 p.m. precisely] the veil of the temple was rent in twain from top to bottom. It was precisely at this hour that the priests were ministering in the temple. You can imagine as they stood before the altar of incense, suddenly and dramatically, they heard an almighty roar as the curtain, the thickness of a hand's breath, sixty feet high and thirty feet wide, was ripped in two from top to bottom. God was watching every detail of the drama on Calvary, and when the work was completed, [He] testified from heaven by rending the veil in two. This hidden hand could not have been that of a man. Only God could have torn it from the top to the bottom.[2]

9. Mark 15:39 and Luke 23:47 tell of yet another miracle that occurred in the heart of a man standing close to the cross. What was it?

>   *Was it for crimes that I have done,*
>
>   *He groaned upon the tree?*
>
>   *Amazing pity! Grace unknown!*
>
>   *And love beyond degree!*
>
>   Isaac Watts

10. According to Mark 15:40–41, what group had followed Jesus, and was lingering near enough to view their Savior on the cross?

These women had served Him and the disciples throughout His ministry. They had given themselves and their money to follow Him (Luke 8:2–3). From their viewpoint they looked on, not willing to take their eyes off the One they loved. They would observe His simple funeral and be ready to minister to His broken body at dawn on the first day of the week. These consecrated women are powerful examples for us to follow.

>   *But drops of grief can ne'er repay,*
>
>   *The debt of love I owe.*
>
>   *Here Lord, I give myself away,*
>
>   *'Tis all that I can do.*
>
>   Isaac Watts

"AND HE BOUGHT FINE LINEN AND TOOK HIM DOWN"

None of the disciples were around to care for Jesus' body. However, from among His enemies God raised up a friend to conduct the funeral of His beloved Son. The high priests would have dumped His body into a common criminal's grave, but centuries earlier Isaiah had revealed He would be buried with the rich (Isaiah 53:9).

11. After reading Mark 15:42–43, John 19:38, and Luke 23:50–51, describe the great man God provided to bury the Savior.

According to John 19:39, what other unlikely assistant helped with the burial?

What special materials did Joseph purchase to wrap around the Lord's battered body (Mark 15:46)? What needful items did Nicodemus provide (John 19:39)?

At His birth there was a just man named Joseph to care for and protect the baby Jesus (Matthew 1:19–24). At His death there was another great Joseph to tenderly care for his broken body. Nicodemus was the first man to hear the words of John 3:16. Perhaps he remembered those words about God giving His only Son as he helped take Jesus' body from the cross. His actions at the cross reveal that he had believed and would never perish. Truly, God's ways are marvelous in our sight!

"HE IS RISEN, HE IS NOT HERE"

In three days and nights Jesus no longer needed Joseph's tomb! An angel tidied it up for Joseph's future use. The expensive linen shroud was folded neatly and laid aside for Joseph. The women would come seeking a dead body in need of sweet spices but would forget the pots of ointments after speaking with a heavenly helper.

12. Read Mark 16:1–7. Why did the devoted women hurry to Jesus' tomb as early as possible?

What obstacle were they prepared to face at the tomb?

In what condition did they find the burial place of Jesus, and who was its new resident?

What startling message did the angel have for them?

To whom were they to share the good news of Jesus' resurrection?

13. Read Mark 16:7 again. What is the significance of the words "as he said unto you"? Review these verses: Mark 9:9–10, 31; 10:33–34.

14. What was the response of the women to the angel's wonderful news (Mark 16:8)?

What was Mary Magdalene's response when the living Lord appeared to her (Mark 16:9–10)?

15. The disciples were together somewhere in Jerusalem. What does Mark 16:10 reveal about them?

How did they receive Mary's consoling message (Mark 16:11)?

For what familiar sin did the risen Lord once again rebuke His disciples (Mark 16:14)?

As a contrast to the persistently unbelieving disciples, read Job 19:25–27. Fifteen hundred years before the amazing events in Jerusalem, a great Old Testament servant announced his faith in a risen redeemer.

16. Who was this servant, and what words of faith did he speak?

"GO YE INTO ALL THE WORLD AND PREACH THE GOSPEL"

Before we conclude Mark, I want to comment on Mark 16:9–20. Some scholars say these verses are not found in the best early manuscripts of Scripture.

> If that were the case, it is inconceivable that Mark would finish his action packed Gospel with the tears of Mark 16:8. The Holy Spirit is not only the Author of the Book He also preserves the Book. Instead of the tears [of verse 8], the final verses of Mark offer the triumph of the resurrection. Furthermore, everything we find in verses 9–16 is in total harmony with the other Gospel writers. No new doctrine is introduced, and no major doctrine is changed or diminished in these verses.[3]

17. According to Mark 16:15, Jesus had a new mission for His men. What was it?

_____

_____

It is wonderful to note here that to "those very men who had so ungratefully forsaken Him and fled, He now said '*Go ye into all the world and preach the Gospel*,' I will trust even you with My message to sinners. Herein is Christ's love."[4] Herein is also hope for all His children who are so prone to wander!

18. Read Mark 16:17–18. What special powers and help did Jesus give to His men before He sent them forth with the message of salvation?

_____

_____

> These signs belonged to the transitional period. The early chapters of the book of Acts are full of such signs. Both Peter and Paul healed the sick and raised the dead. Tongues was common in the early church; it was however, essentially a judgment and a warning sign to the unbelieving Jews. [These gifts] came to an end with the destruction of Jerusalem and the completion of the New Testament.[5]

19. Does Mark 16:16 teach salvation as a combination of faith and works? Support your answer with Scripture.

He is not saying that baptism is necessary to salvation, but that the person who is saved will be baptized. It is the rejection of Christ which brings eternal damnation (John 3:36).[6]

20. Where is our risen, conquering Lord today (Mark 16:19)?

According to Hebrews 7:25, what is He doing for us? What does this mean?

Hebrews 4:14–16 describes a great opportunity for all who know Christ as Savior. Until the temple events in this lesson, no one could exercise such a privilege. What great truth do we find here?

THINK ON THESE THINGS

✛ The story of Christ's death is not altogether a story of brutality and hatred. Don't forget those who were kind to Christ. Don't forget that in that last terrible week Martha and Mary had made Him a meal, and Mary anointed Him with her most precious ointment. One unknown servant also lent Him a donkey; another gave Him his upper room. When the day of His death came, the dedicated women of Galilee and Jerusalem wept over Him, and Joseph of Arimathea boldly requested the privilege of conducting His funeral. Nicodemus assisted Joseph, gratefully providing one hundred pounds of burial spices. And who can forget the supreme kindness of Simon the Cyrenian who carried His cross? When these first-century servants walked onto the pages of Scripture, they left us powerful examples of what it means to willingly surrender all and follow Him.

✛ Jesus' last command to the disciples was very specific: they were
to preach the gospel to every creature. Evangelist D. L. Moody
gave this stirring example of what it means to share the love of
Christ with every creature:

> I can imagine Peter asked Him: "What, Lord ! Shall we offer
> salvation to the men who mocked You and crucified You?"
> And I can imagine Jesus answering him: "Yes, Peter, I want
> you to preach My gospel to everybody beginning at Jerusalem.
> Proclaim salvation to the men who crucified Me. Peter, I'd like
> you to find that man who put the crown of thorns on My head.
> Tell him if he'll take salvation as a gift he shall have a crown
> of glory from Me, and there won't be a thorn in it. Look up
> that Roman soldier who thrust that spear into My side and My
> heart, and tell him there's a nearer way to My heart than that.
> My heart is full of love for his soul. Proclaim salvation to him
> also."[7]

✛ We close the pages of Mark's stirring book with a look, once
again, at Mark 10:45. Here Jesus clearly tells His disciples why
He left heaven's glory to walk with sinners: "For even the Son of
man came not to be ministered unto, but to minister, and to give his
life a ransom for many."

He had everything in heaven, but He willingly surrendered
all of it. Why? To become a servant and to die. When we fully
give ourselves to God, it will mean death. "Death to some of
your desires and plans at least, and death to yourself."[8]

> *Not I but Christ, in lowly, silent labor;*
> *Not I, but Christ in humble, earnest toil;*
> *Christ only Christ, no show, no ostentation!*
> *Christ, only Christ, my all in all to be.*
> *Oh, to be saved from myself dear Lord,*
> *Oh, to be lost in Thee;*
> *Oh, that it may be no more I,*
> *But Christ that lives in me.*
> *Mrs. A. A. Whiddington*

SHADOW SERVANTS

Those Who Served with D. L. Moody—Marianne Adlard

D. L. Moody sailed for England in June 1872. This was not a preaching trip; instead he traveled alone so that he could sit at the feet of some of the godly English Bible teachers such as C. H. Spurgeon and Joseph Parker. He was hungry to gain a deeper knowledge of God's Word. It was a rather long way to go for preaching and Bible study, but Moody was strongly impressed by the Holy Spirit to make the trip. He didn't know there was an invalid woman in North London who was praying for Mr. Moody to minister in her country.

When Moody arrived in England, he began quietly attending preaching services, and his serious study of the Bible began. One evening he attended a prayer meeting at the Old Bailey Court House in London. Pastor John Lessey recognized the evangelist and implored him to preach for him the following Sunday. A very reluctant Moody finally relented, and on the next Lord's Day he was in the pulpit of the New Court Congregational Church, one of the oldest Nonconformist churches in the city.

He received somewhat of a cold shoulder from the congregation, however, and hesitated to return for the evening service. At that service it "seemed, while he was preaching, as if the very atmosphere was charged with the Spirit of God. There came a hush upon all people, and a quick response to his words, though he had not been much in prayer that day, and could not understand it."[9] The response to his invitation was astounding to Moody and Pastor Lessey. So many people came forward that they thought the crowd had misunderstood the invitation, and they doubted about how serious the people were about spiritual things! After the men conferred, they asked those who were truly earnest about salvation to meet the pastor at the church on Monday night.

On that evening, even more inquirers showed up! A mighty revival had begun, and as Moody preached the next ten nights, more than four hundred people professed Christ. The great evangelist knew that such a work came about only through fervent prayer, and he was right! Little did he know that a bedridden young woman named Marianne Adlard had pleaded with God to send Moody to her church even though she was too ill to attend any services. She had read of his Spirit-filled work in Chicago and hungered for such a life-changing ministry in her church.

When told of the praying invalid Moody asked about her, and he did not stop asking until he was sitting by her bedside thanking her for praying without ceasing on his behalf. Together they praised God for such a mighty moving of His Spirit in the New Court Church and for God bringing Moody over four thousand miles because of her continual presence at the throne of grace.

The great evangelist and the prayer warrior became friends in the Lord, and Marianne would later tell her new, young pastor G. Campbell Morgan that she prayed every day for Moody until he went home to heaven in 1899. She also began a ministry of prayer for Pastor Morgan. He later told her story and dedicated his book *The Practice of Prayer* to her memory.

Both D. L. Moody and pastor and author G. Campbell Morgan never doubted the power of Miss Marianne Adlard's prayers. Until his death, Moody believed his 1872 visit to Britain was prompted by the Holy Spirit all because of the mighty prayers of a young suffering prayer warrior. He and Morgan often rejoiced because of God's countless servants who are content to faithfully serve in the shadows, thereby enabling others who labor in public to do their work for God.

Notes

LESSON 1

1. Warren Wiersbe, *Be Diligent* (Wheaton, IL: Victor Books, 1987), 20.

LESSON 2

1. Victor Maxwell, *The Authentic Servant* (Greenville, SC: Ambassador, 1996), 35.
2. John Phillips, *Exploring the Gospel of Mark* (Grand Rapids, MI: Kregel, 2004), 60.
3. Maxwell, 35–36.

LESSON 3

1. J. D. Jones, *Commentary on Mark* (Grand Rapids, MI: Kregel, 1992), 79.
2. John MacArthur, *New Testament Commentary, Matthew 8–15* (Winona Lake, IN: BMH, 1987), 339.
3. Edward H. Bartlett, *Mrs. Bartlett and Her Class at the Metropolitan Tabernacle* (London: Passmore and Alabaster, 1877), 69.

LESSON 4

1. Phillips, 111.
2. J. C. Ryle, *Mark: Expository Thoughts on the Gospels* (Wheaton, IL: Crossway, 1993), 78.
3. Fred Donehoo, *Serving the Servant* (Greenville, SC: BJU Press, 2009), 69.
4. Ryle, 81.
5. Susannah Spurgeon and Joseph Harrald, *C. H. Spurgeon Autobiography*, vol. 2 (Carlisle, PA: Banner of Truth, 1987), 163.

LESSON 5

1. Jones, 209.
2. Charles Edwards, *Treasury of Daily Devotions*, July 2 (Greenville, SC: Ambassador Productions, 2003).

LESSON 6

1. D. Edmond Hiebert, *The Gospel of Mark* (Greenville, SC: Bob Jones University Press, 1994), 193.
2. Ryle, 161.
3. Wiersbe, 74.
4. Hiebert, 220.
5. *Life Application Study Bible* (Wheaton, IL: Tyndale, 1989), 1666.
6. Lewis Drummond, *Spurgeon, Prince of Preachers* (Grand Rapids, MI: Kregel, 1992), 322.
7. Drummond, 607.
8. C. H. Spurgeon, *The Treasury of David*, vol. 1 (McLean, VA: MacDonald, n.d.), n.p.

LESSON 7

1. Hiebert, 235.
2. C. H. Spurgeon, *The Gospel of the Kingdom* (Pasadena, TX: Pilgrim, 1978), 138.
3. Donehoo, 111.
4. Elizabeth R. Skoglund, *Wounded Heroes* (Grand Rapids, MI: Baker, 1992), 94.

LESSON 8

1. Jones, 339.
2. James A. Brooks, *Mark, The New American Commentary* (Nashville, TN: Broadman Press, 1991), 158.
3. Frederick G. Warne, *George Muller—The Modern Apostle of Faith* (Bristol, England: Burleigh, 1911), 121.

LESSON 9

1. A. B. Simpson, quoted in *Streams in the Desert*, April 28, Mrs. Charles E. Cowman (Ulrichsville, OH: Barbour, n.d.).
2. Charles H. Spurgeon, *Morning and Evening* (Grand Rapids, MI: Zondervan Publishing House, 1971), 436.
3. S. Pearce Carey, *William Carey* (London, England: Wakeman Trust, 1993), 84.
4. Carey, 112.

LESSON 10

1. Jones, 497.
2. *Biblical Viewpoint: Focus on Mark* (Greenville, SC: Bob Jones University, 1977), 125.
3. Donehoo, 190.
4. John Henry Jowett, *Things That Are Needful* (Grand Rapids, MI: Baker, 1977), 23.
5. Charles H. Spurgeon, *Spurgeon's Expository Encyclopedia*, vol. 10 (Grand Rapids, MI: Baker, 1985), 360–61.
6. M. Geraldine Guinness, *The Story of the China Inland Mission* (London: Morgan and Scott, 1893), 279.
7. M. Geraldine Guinness, *The Story of the China Inland Mission*, vol. 2 (London: Morgan and Scott, 1894), 114–15.

LESSON 11

1. Jones, 558.
2. Ryle, 240.
3. Phillips, 324.
4. Ryle, 250.
5. Dr. and Mrs. Howard Taylor, *Hudson Taylor and the China Inland Mission*, Vol. 2 (Singapore: OMF Books, 1998), 72.
6. Isobel Kuhn, *In the Arena* (Singapore: OMF Books, 1988), 37.
7. Jim Cromarty, *It Is Not Death to Die* (Ross-shire, Great Britain: Christian Focus, 2001), 207.

LESSON 12

1. Charles H. Spurgeon, *The Gospel of the Kingdom* (Pasadena, TX: Pilgrim Publications, 1974), 248.
2. Maxwell, 158.
3. Maxwell, 167.
4. Andrew A. Bonar, *Heavenly Springs* (Carlisle, PA: Banner of Truth, 1986), 96.
5. Phillips, 348.
6. J. Vernon McGee, *Thru the Bible with J. Vernon McGee*, vol. 4 (Pasadena, CA: Thru the Bible Radio, 1983), 236.
7. Charles H. Spurgeon, *My Sermon Notes*, vol 3 (Grand Rapids, MI: Baker, 1984), 191.
8. Elisabeth Elliot, *A Lamp for My Feet* (Ann Arbor, MI: Servant Publications, 1985), 39.
9. William R. Moody, *The Life of Moody by His Son* (Chicago, IL: Revell, 1900), 152.